Insiders
& COMPANY
The New Artisans of Interior Design

gestalten

Contents

Preface		004
La Manufacture Cogolin	Flooring Rugs	012
Dinesen	Flooring	018
Addresses	FLOORING	028
Addresses	FLOORING Rugs	029
Københavns Møbelsnedkeri	Built-Ins	030
Victoria Wilmotte	Furniture Metal	036
Sebastian Cox	Furniture Wood	042
Marcin Rusak	Furniture Resin	046
Cristina Celestino	Decorations Tiles	052
Geoffrey Preston	Decorations Stucco	056
Crosby Studios	Built-Ins	064
Houlès	Decorations Textiles	068
Anna Karlin	Furniture Wood	072
Roll & Hill	Lighting	074
Addresses	LIGHTING	078
Addresses	DECORATIONS Stone, Metal & Glass	081
Marta Sala	Furniture Upholstery	082
The Nanz Company	Decorations Hardware	086
Fromental	Decorations Textiles	090
Eligo Studio	Furniture Wood	094
Addresses	FURNITURE Vintage & Re-Editions	096
Valentin Loellmann	Furniture Wood	098
Clarence House	Decorations Textiles	104
Soane Britain	Furniture Rattan	108
Addresses	FURNITURE Wood & Natural Fibers	114
Muller van Severen	Furniture Metal	118
Garnier & Linker	Furniture Wood	122
RENS	Flooring Rugs	124
DWA Design Studio	Furniture Stone	128
Jende Posamenten Manufaktur	Decorations Textiles	132
Anchor Ceramics	Decorations Tiles	136

Amy Somerville	Furniture Upholstery 140
Addresses	FURNITURE Upholstery & Beds 148
Tadeáš Podracký	Tableware 152
Garde Hvalsøe	Built-Ins 154
Roi du Lac	Decorations Textiles 158
Charles Dedman	Furniture Wood 162
Jorge Penadés	Lighting 164
Laboratorio Paravicini	Tableware 168
Addresses	TABLEWARE 172
Schotten & Hansen	Flooring 174
Savoir Beds	Furniture Upholstery 178
Braquenié	Decorations Textiles 184
Addresses	DECORATIONS Textiles & Wallpaper 192
Germans Ermičs	Furniture Glass 196
Lison de Caunes	Furniture Straw 200
John Sankey	Furniture Upholstery 208
Ateliers Zelij	Decorations Tiles 212
Addresses	KITCHENS & BATHROOMS & TILES 216
Addresses	DECORATIONS Paints 219
Voutsa	Decorations Textiles 220
Nymphenburg	Tableware 224
llot llov	Furniture Wood 230
Bloc Studios	Furniture Marble 234
Addresses	FURNITURE Metal & Glass, Stone 242
Addresses	BUILT-INS 244
Addresses	RADIATORS & FIREPLACES 244
Bonnemazou Cambus	Decorations Hardware 246
Atelier Dialect	Built-Ins 250
Joseph Walsh	Furniture Wood 252
cc-tapis	Flooring Rugs 256
Golem	Decorations Tiles 264
Index	 270

A Moment of Appreciation

There are, as usual, two camps: one in which craftspeople are viewed as trade workers, associated with malfunctions and defects that need to be fixed, whether that's the washing machine, a leaky pipe, or some other bathroom nightmare; the other camp sees craftspeople as the creators of objects that, ideally, won't need fixing for a long time to come, if ever. Their pieces are high quality and age with dignity—they are made to last a lifetime. We are part of the second camp, and celebrate skilled artisans, adept technicians, and masterful makers within these following pages.

We, the consumers of today, conscious fans of quality and astonishing aesthetics, seek out high-quality products that have a history. We want to know where the materials come from, how they were treated and, above all, who turns them into the products we buy. Pierric De Coster, co-founder of design studio Atelier Dialect (pp. 250 – 251) thinks that the attentive buyer is driven by "the desire to get everything right the first time." He goes on to say that people just don't like going to furniture stores any more. "There seems to have been a shift in recent years; this interest in craftsmanship, longevity, and quality is new. Today's generation pays a lot more attention to those things than, let's say, our grandparents—which means that most of our customers are just as young as we are." It also means that an entire industry has been given a new lease on life, with this interest no longer limited to a small group of design enthusiasts.

WE WANT TO KNOW WHERE THE MATERIALS COME FROM, HOW THEY WERE TREATED AND ESPECIALLY BY WHOM.

Give Thanks for Crafts

The term "craft" can refer to a variety of very different disciplines—from fixing cars to working as a cooper, bell founder, furrier, brush maker, or carpenter. Until industrialization there were guilds for every necessity: the production of a chair, for instance, included upholsterers, weavers, and turners. What unites all of these professions is a passion for quality, and an expertise that is passed on from master to apprentice. If we look at the world of furnishings, we see that the crafts themselves are often nothing new—quite the opposite, in fact. Plasterers, passementerie makers, ceramicists, weavers, and stonemasons have all existed for centuries. What is new, however, is the desire to unmask how the products are manufactured. Handmade products have a higher status than those made by machines. In the second half of the last century, a time when Italian designer Gaetano Pesce made a chair from foam that could be vacuum-compressed to 5 percent of its original volume, the prevailing opinion was quite different. Mass-production for everyone was new and novel. Pesce's design was exciting in its ability to be efficiently stored and transported. But today, as we have become more and more consumed by our touchscreens and apps, the value of custom-made products is at a premium.

When it comes to promoting crafts, some countries invest more than others. Germany is one of them, as is Italy, France, and the United Kingdom. Mention the English countryside, and most people imagine gently rolling hills crisscrossed by low stone walls. These walls are the product of a centuries-old method that was at risk of dying out. To save it, the British government launched a funding program to train the next generation in making these walls, a skill that requires expertly layering nothing more than stone fragments. The initiative has made it possible to learn an ancient craft in the modern world.

Designers and Craftspeople Unite

Craftspeople are free to specialize in production only, leaving the design side to a designer, or they can instead choose to do both jobs themselves. Everyone applies their talent in different ways. Peter Paul Rubens had his painter's workshop, Walter Gropius declared the unity of art and crafts at his Bauhaus art school, and Damien Hirst has his employees cast his bronze statues. Many of today's young designers both devise and make their products. They benefit from design school skills still fresh in their minds, and may find their return to the workbench born of necessity, not yet having a network of producers to bring their designs to life.

Craft workshops are essentially the craftsperson's elder sibling. Here, too, the focus is on producing things by hand, but with the support of a company. Designers and craft workshops often cross paths. Take Marta Sala, a Milan-based furniture creator (pp. 82–85). Her products are designed by renowned architects such as Lazzarini Pickering Architetti, and produced by long-established craft businesses in Brienza. Sala is discerning when selecting those she partners with along each step in the process, creating a highly skilled supergroup to support her vision. Craftspeople are the most intelligent of all, she says, because "they have to find solutions to all the things that no one else thinks about."

When Lulu Lytle, creative director and founder of the British furniture company Soane (pp. 108–113), needed to find suitable craftspeople, she turned to the archives of the Crafts Council, a U.K. agency for contemporary crafts. She spent days scouring the old records for blacksmiths and saddlers who had the skills to turn her own traditional designs into modern-day products. In the end, she created a fascinating map showing the regional distribution of the individual crafts.

PREFACE
by Sally Fuls

THERE IS ANOTHER REWARD THAT MONEY CAN'T BUY: THE PLEASURE IN CHOOSING QUALITY IN DESIGN, FUNCTION, AND WORKMANSHIP.

Quality before Quantity

If you explore the design industry today and ask an interior designer about the importance of luxury and status in their work, you will likely hear a variation on the same answer: "This is not about money and prestige. The most important things are craftsmanship and, above all, quality." But this is ignoring an important fact: good craftsmanship comes at a price. And the ability to pay that price makes a statement. Handmade products involve highly specialized skills, high-grade materials, modes of production that are kind to people and animals, and a huge amount of time. Therefore, one cannot pretend that money doesn't play a role.

The people who built the Beelitzer Heilstätten, a disused lung hospital in northern Germany, reframe this cost well: the most expensive things are always the cheapest in the end because they last longer. And indeed, about 130 years after the hospital was built, it has stood the test of time. They chose Villeroy & Boch tiles, for instance, and had the water pipes made out of copper. Today, people have been caught sneaking into the site to steal old materials for use in new products.

PREFACE

Crafting the Future

So, has true craftsmanship escaped extinction? We hope so. Brands such as Soane train their own producers to ensure that skillsets will be passed on; wooden floor manufacturer Dinesen (pp. 18–27) is investing in new methods and locations; and plasterer Geoffrey Preston (pp. 56–63) is priming a successor—after the self-taught craftsman became the United Kingdom's best-known stucco and plaster designer. The important art of apprenticeship is alive and well among craftspeople and craft workshops. The range of crafts on display in *Insiders & Company* shines a light on the future. From young designers who manufacture their own products, to small and medium-sized craft workshops that are bringing traditional methods into the modern world, to large companies that value workmanship over the speed of the assembly line—the community here is fusing tradition with innovation, is passionate about handmade products, and is pursuing nothing less than absolute excellence. So, dear readers, when it comes to furnishing your own homes, we ask only one thing of you: Don't do it yourself. Each and every page of this book will help you understand why.

Aside from a wise, upfront investment, there is another reward that money can't buy: the pleasure in choosing quality in design, function, and workmanship. In the past, there was no alternative to handmade products. Today, we can choose whether we buy something handmade or not. Soane's Lulu Lytle believes that great craftsmanship comes at a price. "It is incumbent on us to try and make pieces really beautifully at a price that makes them as available as possible to as many people as possible. But we must also be mindful that there is a cost to making things on a very high level. And we can't be shy in acknowledging that in the craftsmen we choose to work with." Nevertheless, in order to optimize costs and processes, Soane might adapt a technique that has nothing to do with furniture making. For instance, the small parts used in Soane lamps are made by a company that specializes in precision medical equipment.

Anyone who cannot afford these products or who simply chooses not to incur the cost can scour local flea markets for a good find. A chair that has survived the past 50 years will presumably last another 50—pieces with history, and a good story, are out there to be found.

Purple chevron pattern (below) produced on a traditional jacquard loom (left) from the Jardin Intérieur collection designed by India Mahdavi. The Ondulation pattern is from the Ombres et Anamorphoses flat-weave collection (left page).

Handmade Rugs That Loom Large

La Manufacture Cogolin in France has been producing hand-woven rugs for an elite clientele for nearly a century. Thanks to the vision of textiles entrepreneur Jean Lauer, who ran the company from 1928 until his death in 1962, the workshop gained international acclaim, its exclusive hand-knotted and woven carpets adorning the floors of luxury residences, embassies, and palaces. La Manufacture Cogolin experienced a rebirth in 2010 when it joined House of Tai Ping, a group of leading carpet brands. The color palette was reworked to comprise 200 vibrant colors (in addition to custom colors), and new materials were introduced. The nineteenth-century jacquard looms were restored, where one weaver might work for two months on a single made-to-order rug. The workshop also collaborates with ateliers in Nepal, where hand-knot weaving is still performed. In addition to reissuing historical designs, the company continues to look to the future, creating new sophisticated collections, often in collaboration with celebrated designers such as India Mahdavi and Charles Zana. ✕

Cogolin's skilled artisans use four different traditional rug-making techniques: flat weave (above: Lacis), pattern weave (right: Isotopie), textured weave (right page: Variamen designed by Charles Zana), and hand knotting.

Dinesen
Danish Delights

The forest has served as a source of inspiration for the Dinesen family since 1898, resulting in exquisite wood planks that preserve nature's riches while telling the story of its trees.

Dinesen uses raw wood from majestic Douglas firs and characterful oak trees. Douglas firs can be found in the Black Forest, Germany (above), among other places.

Choosing a floor for a home is like tuning an instrument—only when it feels harmonious and balanced can the rest of the space hit the right notes. In that sense, the floor anchors the mood in a space. With wooden planks from Danish specialist Dinesen, this foundation will feel strong and serene—in the moment and for generations to come. The family-owned business, founded in 1898, is still based in the small town of Jels, and has aged beautifully while keeping step with modern times. Now led by 4th-generation family members Thomas Dinesen and his wife Heidi, the company strikes a harmonious cord between craftsmanship and the latest in technology.

How do you feel about the legacy you have inherited?
It is a wonderful feeling to sense the powerful values and traditions that are embedded in our long history. My great-grandfather was interested in technical solutions, my grandfather in manufacturing, and my father in creativity. And they all loved wood. I myself studied forestry and worked in the forest for nine years. In 1983, I met my wife Heidi in a traffic accident. We actually decided together to take over the family business, which we did in 1989.

How has the production of Dinesen planks evolved since you joined the business?

Over time, we have optimized and expanded our manufacturing process. In 2017, we opened a new oak factory where the latest technology makes the production a little easier. But even today, it is the human element that ensures the quality. Every single plank passes through at least 10 pairs of hands on their journey through our production facilities. We have a dedicated quality control team that is specialized in knots. It's normal for an 80- to 120-year-old tree to have a few knots that are no longer fresh. We remove them and carefully replace them with a suitable knot. This helps us also to use as much as possible from a felled tree.

You use oak, fir, and Douglas fir wood for your products. Why those types?

All three species have a light, Scandinavian expression. They make for a quiet and discreet floor—and a special foundation for furniture, design, and art.

A WOODEN FLOOR CAN BRING A UNIQUELY HUMAN, NATURAL TOUCH TO OTHERWISE COLD AND MINIMALIST ARCHITECTURE.

Above, a huge trunk from a 111-year-old Douglas tree in the Dinesen showroom. Dinesen Douglas used in a private residence (left and right page bottom) and, Dinesen Douglas GrandPattern finished with an anthracite grey oil in the Copenhagen restaurant Kadeau (right page top).

From where do you source your wood?
We import most of our wood from Germany, but we also work with other European countries with a century-long tradition for sustainable forestry. Germany, for example, benefits from very strict forest law brought into force many years ago. And it is one of the countries in Europe where the amount of wood growing back is actually larger than the amount harvested.

How much time goes by from cutting down a tree until the planks are ready to be shipped to your customer's home?
It is quite a lengthy process, between 3 and 6 months, or even longer, depending on species, lengths and widths, and, of course, the size of the project. All Dinesen planks are unique and the expression of the planks varies according to the customers' wishes. Some prefer a classic look, while others like a more natural expression with more knots. We select each tree in the forest based on criteria such as straightness, growth rings, knots, and harmony. The large trunks are then cut into planks, which are stacked with space for air to circulate. After the air-drying follows the kiln-drying. After the quality check, the planks are sanded one more time to

A KNOT IS THE PART OF A BRANCH THAT IS EMBEDDED IN THE TRUNK, AND IT IS TESTIMONY TO THE HISTORY OF THE TREE.

Dinesen Douglas flooring inside of the masting houses, where the Danish navy's masts used to be stored over the winter. Today, they house a number of design studios (above). Dinesen HeartOak planks are used for wall cladding in the private home and studio of Danish photographer Peter Krasilnikoff (right page).

ensure a pleasant texture. At the end comes a final manual and visual check of quality and appearance, until the planks are ready to be packed.

They look as though they would feel almost soft to the touch. How do you achieve this?
We keep the surface natural, so it's very tactile. You get an irresistible desire to let the hand slide over the surface to feel the beautiful unevenness and structure. In particular, a soap-treated floor has a silky-smooth, yet hard-wearing finish.

How long can one expect a Dinesen floor to last?
They are made to last for generations. But they are not intended to continue looking like new, but should be characterized by the life lived in the house. However, the better the floor is looked after with a soap or oil finish, the more beautiful the planks will patinate.

How does the wood react in a home?
It expands and contracts continually with changes in air humidity and temperature. If the indoor climate remains completely stable throughout the year, the planks will remain dimensionally stable. But even with expensive climate systems, this is hard to achieve. Therefore, periodical contraction gaps should be accepted so that the floor can respond to the change of seasons. Indeed, some customers deliberately choose to keep these gaps bigger than we recommend—they like that very clean-lined look.

What do you think a wooden floor adds to a home?
It can bring a uniquely human, natural touch to what might otherwise be fairly cold and minimalist architecture. Our planks contribute to a very special ambience and let concrete, glass, and steel appear more beautiful. I personally love a certain human aspect of wood. A tree can reveal hidden secrets once the trunk is opened. And no two trees or planks are completely identical. They all have their differences and their own distinct personality. Also, when you treat the tree and the wood with care and respect, it will give you a lot of beauty and joy in return.

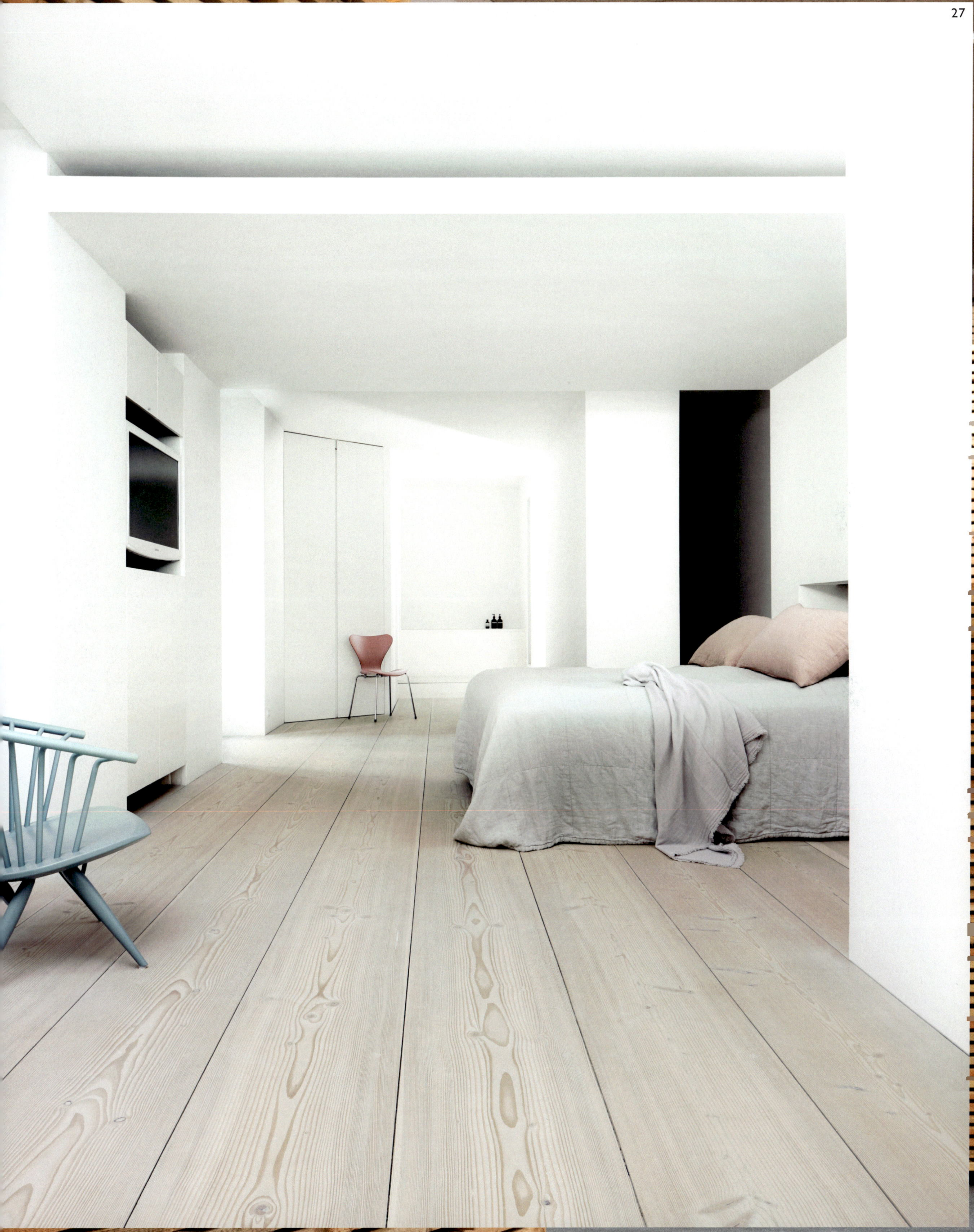

Dinesen

Flooring

Boleflor
Amsterdam, Netherlands
Production of naturally curved hardwood flooring.
___bolefloor.com

Bolon
Ulricehamn, Sweden
Sustainable, woven vinyl flooring.
___bolon.com

Ceramiche Refin
Casalgrande, Italy
Porcelain stoneware wall and floor tiles.
___refin-fliesen.de

Dinesen
Rødding, Denmark
Quality wooden floorboards in oak and Douglas fir, in a range of finishes.
___dinesen.com
pp. 18–27

DLW
Bietigheim-Bissingen, Germany
Vinyl, laminate, and linoleum floor coverings since more than 130 years.
___dlw.de

Fagus
Boffzen, Germany
Produces and lays quality floorboards and parquet flooring.
___kassettenboden.de

Forbo
Assendelft, Netherlands
Sustainable floor coverings, including linoleum, vinyl and carpet tiles.
___forbo.com

Lindner Group
Arnstorf, Germany
Sustainably raised flooring systems, available in a variety of wood, metallic, and textile coverings.
___lindner-group.com

Mafi
Schneegattern, Austria
Natural, air-cured, and oiled floorboards in a range of woods and designs, metal and textile flooring systems
___mafi.com

Nolte
Wolfsburg, Germany
Production and installation of a wide range of flooring solutions, from textile and elastic floor coverings to cork, laminate, and engineered parquet floors, for private homes and businesses.
___nolte-ausbau.de

Parador
Coesfeld, Germany
Laminate, parquet and vinyl flooring systems.
___parador.de

Parkett Dietrich
Wuppertal, Germany
Quality parquet flooring, inlays, and stairs in a wide range of woods and shades, also for bathrooms.
___parkett-dietrich.de

Richard Woods
London, United Kingdom
Bold, colorful, and cartoonish wood-cut printed floor coverings.
___richardwoodsstudio.com

Schotten & Hansen
Peiting, Germany
Naturally treated wooden floorboards.
___schotten-hansen.com
pp. 174–177

Traco Manufactur
Bad Langensalza, Germany
Quarry and manufacture limestone, sandstone, and travertine paving.
___traco-manufactur.de

Flooring Rugs

cc-tapis
Milan, Italy
Design and production of contemporary, one-of a kind hand-knotted rugs with geometric patterns.
___cc-tapis.com
pp. 256–263

Christopher Farr
London, United Kingdom
Rugs, produced in a variety of styles, often in collaboration with renowned artists and architects.
___christopherfarr.com

Danskina
Amsterdam, Netherlands
Modern, minmalistic made-to-order rugs.
___danskina.com

Diurne
Paris, France
Hand-woven and custom-made rugs with an artistic touch, inspired by Art Deco.
___www.diurne.com

Gan
Valencia, Spain
Hand-woven rugs with eye-catching textures and patterns, also for outdoors.
___gan-rugs.com

Golran
Milan, Italy
Hand-knotted rugs, contemporary and traditional collections by, for instance, Dimore Studio or Piero Lissoni.
___golran.com

Jan Kath
Bochum, Germany
Hand-knotted rugs that combine classic oriental elements with contemporary minimalist design.
___jan-kath.de

Joa Herrenknecht
Berlin, Germany
Colorful, geometric textured rugs. Also offers furniture, ceramics, table-ware, and lighting.
___joa-herrenknecht.com

La Manufacture Cogolin
Cogolin, France
Hand-knotted and jacquard rugs by Jean-Michel Frank, David Hicks, or Jean Cocteau.
___manufacturecogolin.com
pp. 12–17

Luke Irwin
London, United Kingdom
Hand-knotted custom-made rugs—from Berber carpets to Ikat patterns.
___lukeirwin.com

RENS
Eindhoven, Netherlands
Manually re-dyed carpets, produced in collaboration with DESSO, using their end-of-line collections.
___madebyrens.com
pp. 124–127

Nodus
Milan, Italy
Limited-edition, high-design, and bespoke rugs in bright colors and eclectic patterns, produced in collaboration with a variety of international designers, such as Studio Job.
___nodusrug.it

Reuber Henning
Berlin, Germany
Hand-knotted rugs, produced in Nepal, using traditional techniques and Tibetan wool.
___reuberhenning.de

Tai Ping
Hong Kong, China
High-quality carpets, produced with a range of techniques, including hand-tufting, pass-tufting, hand-knotting, hand-weaving, machine-tufting, robot-tufting, Axminster and Wilton.
___houseoftaiping.com

The Rug Company
London, United Kingdom
Traditionally produced carpets, designed in collaboration with a range of creatives, as, for example, fashion designer Alexander McQueen
___therugcompany.com

Tufenkian
New York, United States
Fair trade carpets in a wide range of colors and styles.
___tufenkian.com

cc-tapis

Neo-Nordic furniture by Københavns Møbelsnedkeri (KBH), co-founded in 2006 by Kim Dolva (right page). Above, the KBH Dedar sofa, part of their New Classics collection.

Custom-built in Copenhagen

Kim Dolva went from building guitars to graphic design before he enrolled in a five-year training program in cabinetry. In 2006, he and fellow classmate Søren Jespersen launched their own cabinetry business in Copenhagen, Københavns Møbelsnedkeri. Their passion for craft finds expression in their elegant and highly detailed creations for an increasingly international clientele. "We try to create modern design classics with an enormous attention to details," says Dolva. "We are influenced by the Danish golden age of furniture design, Japanese joinery, American industrialism, and southern European decor." Over the years, Københavns Møbelsnedkeri has expanded its team and expertise beyond the realm of wood to include metal, glass, leather, and stone. In addition to custom builds, the manufacturers recently launched a production collection available through select dealers around the world. Says Dolva, "My partners and I have a deal that every day is about becoming better. Because the only way our company can have a strong position in the world is to deliver quality work every single time." ✗

KBH combined dark and light fumed oak with brass and glass to create this custom Old School cabinetry (left page).

Industrial Allure

Victoria Wilmotte's design process is akin to that of a sculptor, "measuring volumes and empty spaces, finding the perfect angle or curve, and polishing the surfaces to achieve the precise structure, haptics, and light refraction." Wilmotte was born in Paris in 1985, the youngest child of esteemed architect Jean-Michel Wilmotte. After studying interior design at École Camondo in Paris, she earned her master's degree in product design at the Royal College of Art in London, before returning to Paris in 2008 to launch her design studio. Her work reveals a fascination with contrasting surfaces, such as steel with natural stone or resins, as well as precision techniques that enable clear lines, complex forms, and perfect proportions. She calls her studio the VW Factory, a nod to her passion for the industrial world. "I like factories, all the hidden elements that are in the background and are only functional. There is beauty in their simplicity, in the obvious way they work, in their shape." ✕

The table landscape with Guéridon Cristall tables in black and sandblasted white glass was designed for Coedition, and the White Chip trestles and table are made of Corian with an anodized aluminum base (this page). Wilmotte at work in her studio, elevating everyday objects to works of art with her Jasperware Carafe series and Corian Y Lamps (right page).

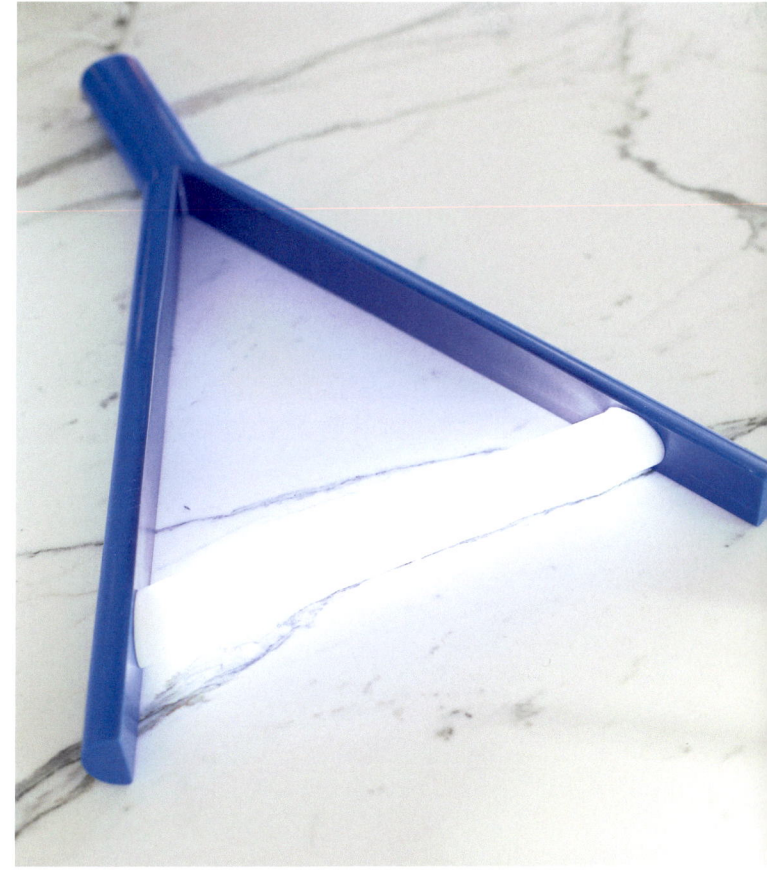

Timber Timbre

Since 2010, Sebastian Cox has dedicated himself to making furniture that reveals the inherent beauty of his materials, which are almost exclusively sustainably and locally sourced British hardwoods. With a studio and workshop in southeast London, Cox follows a philosophy he put forth in 2010 for his master's thesis in sustainable design at Lincoln University: "traditional as radical." As he explains, "I really believe that many of the material challenges we face in society can be overcome by combining an ancient approach to materials and design, with the amazing technological and scientific advances of today." One of his collections is made with hand-coppiced hazel, a byproduct of a traditional forest management practice in which trees are cut down every several years so they regrow quickly and abundantly. A range of small accessories ensures that no wood goes to waste. With an eye on the future, Cox has also set up a biofacture lab with designer Ninela Ivanova, growing and designing compostable furniture with a tree fungus called mycelium. ✕

The Bayleaf Settle is made with solid and woven English chestnut. Behind it to the left, the Mop Stick ladder is made from hand-coppiced Kentish hazel wedged between solid English ash supports (above).

"William Morris is one of my greatest influences, not just in relation to the aesthetic of my work, but also the ethos. His vision for beautiful and totally democratic design is something I dream of realizing through my own work," says Cox.

A Floral Affair

Marcin Rusak spent two years researching the potential of using flowers, a fleeting source of beauty, in creating durable, valuable goods.

"The human race seems to have an enduring obsession with flowers," notes Marcin Rusak, whose multidisciplinary approach builds on his studies in the humanities, art, and design in Warsaw, Eindhoven, and London. For his collection of furniture and lighting created with resin-encased flowers, the London-based designer was inspired by his family's history as flower growers in Warsaw, as well as by the sight of abandoned flowers at a London flower market. "Once flowers fulfill our decorative or symbolic needs, they become an unwanted and discarded reminiscence of life. Treated and processed, they regain some significance and become part of a work which either refers to their very temporary nature, or they are used as decoration itself," he says. For his material Flora Temporaria, flowers suspended in resin produce an intriguing depth. As the petals age, they slightly change in volume, creating what he describes as "silver voids of light around their structures." His material Flora Perma comes out of a non-aging process that reveals cross-sections of flowers contrasting with black resin for a stone-like quality. ✕

Each piece is composed like a painting: flowers and leaves are chosen for their sculptural qualities and colors, and translated into the material only when the effect is satisfactory.

The Tale of Tiles

Milan-based designer Cristina Celestino carefully considers shape, form, geometry, and material when handcrafting her ceramic and porcelain tiles. Her Plumage range of textured tiles for BottegaNove looks to birds' feathers and builds on artisanal traditions in Vicenza, where the firm is located. Her Giardino all'Italiana tile range for Fornace Brioni takes terracotta from its historically rustic application and shifts it toward a contemporary context. Inspired by Renaissance gardens, which sought to "design nature," she creates a landscape of geometric shapes abstracted from meadows, rows of trees, and lakes. After earning a degree in architecture at the University of Venice in 2005, Celestino worked for various architectural firms before launching Attico Design Studio in 2010. Her designs come from both her own research-driven projects and collaborations with brands like Fendi or Tonelli Design. For Celestino, the work is about "exploring and assimilating the beauty surrounding us in order to translate it into real projects, creating interiors and objects that have a contemporary attitude." ✕

Celestino and her Giardino all'Italiana terracotta flooring and wall covering collection for Fornace Brioni (left). Feather-inspired patterns on a handcrafted ceramic vase (above) and tiles for BottegaNove (right page).

Tile forms at Fornace Brioni in Gonzaga, northern Italy, where terracotta tiles are produced exclusively by hand (this page). BottegaNove plumage tile sheets, manually cast in plaster molds and hand finished by artisans in Nove, a town near Venice famous for its artistic pottery (right page).

Preston studied sculpture at Hornsey College of Art in London and trained as a stonemason and carver. He set up his workshop in Devon in 2000.

Geoffrey Preston

The Master of Plaster

From small relief panels to exuberant Rococo ceilings, Geoffrey Preston brings walls, ceilings, and gardens to life with his exquisite hand-modeled stucco and cast plasterwork.

Interior decoration has been unfairly criticized for being a superficial matter. When it comes to plaster and stucco work, there is some truth to this suggestion. Both forms of ceiling and wall decoration are added once all the major architectural work in the room has already been finished. When admiring the work of Geoffrey Preston, Britain's most renowned and respected artisan in this field, one senses that his pieces have a quality that can't be achieved with an interest in looks alone. With a vast knowledge of the craft's history, Preston revives stucco and plasterwork in the United Kingdom by producing original designs that connect to traditional aesthetics, but with a zest for the contemporary.

When did you discover your interest in stucco?
I started out as a sculptor and am also trained as a stone mason. Back then, my friends and I worked with the influential Professor Robert Baker, who revived the use of lime in the conservation of stonework on buildings' exteriors. In churches and other historic buildings, I learned to repair carved modeling with a putty lime aggregate mix. In the early 1990s, I led the team that created the hand-modeled stucco at Uppark House—the first major stucco project that had been done in England since at least the very early nineteenth century.

So the craft needed to be rediscovered?
Yes, all the stucco skills had to be relearned for this. Following that, there was another restoration project at Prior Park College in Bath that involved restoring 36 eighteenth-century stucco patterns. So, during the early 1990s, I gained a lot of experience in modeling in stucco and learning the eighteenth-century styles. After another few years, I set up our workshop to work independently with my own commissions.

Do you still do restorations?
All my work is original now. People in England show quite a love for the classical, Georgian period. Sometimes clients want to commission a ceiling sympathetic to the kind of house they have. That can be an original Georgian building or a house by one of the contemporary classical architects. It's the feeling they wish to have in their houses that then informs my designs. I think some of my clients are out of love for contemporary architecture and design—traditional elements can be much more harmonious. And figurative art is enjoying a moment of revival too.

Preston leads his team of skilled modelers at his workshop in Devon, where everything is done by hand. Plasterwork is first modeled in clay, then a silicone mold is taken from it and used to make a cast in plaster.

What are the main differences between stucco and plaster?

With stucco, you would have your walls and ceilings plastered. In historic times, these were lime mortars, used on lime and finished up finely with three coats of plaster. Ceiling decorations are being modeled or cast in the lime plaster, as was done in the fifteenth, sixteenth, and seventeenth centuries. At one point in the seventeenth century, Italian sculptors began to add gypsum to the lime mortar, creating a plastic material for modeling. Gypsum has the advantage—unlike lime, which will crack and needs to be looked after while drying—that it sets off the modeled work, which is ideal for fine modeling. After you make up your mix, you can work with it for between four to six hours, so you need a clear vision of your design. And you model the work in situ.

And plaster?

In England, in the late eighteenth century, architects like Robert Adam began to work on the designs of the ceiling. Elements of their ceiling designs derived from quite shallow relief work studied in Greece and Italy. These had repetitive elements in them that lent themselves to casting. At about the same time, gypsum was increasingly used in pottery, and became more readily available. So techniques of casting in gypsum became more widely known. My decorative plaster panels are made in my workshop. The process starts with a large sheet of melamine on which I put my design; and then I model the design in clay. This is followed by making a mold and cast from that, which results in a big sheet of plaster with the decoration on it, about 18 mm thick. This is taken into a house and screwed up onto the ceiling.

> WHEN I SEE A CEILING WITH NOTHING ON IT EXCEPT LIGHT FITTINGS IT FEELS LIKE IT IS MISSING SOMETHING.

Each work is unique—there is no molding or casting—in the rare art of stucco, made from lime, gypsum, and a binder, mixed to a putty consistency and then modeled into shape with small metal tools as it sets.

SUCCESSFUL MODELING USES TRADITIONAL SHAPES IN A NEW WAY.

Do you work more with plaster or stucco?
We mostly do cast plaster work, which means I model the work in clay and then cast it. Stucco work is more expensive for the client; it takes much longer and you have to work in situ. In a way, stucco is a bit like fresco: it has the same limitations and advantages. They share a brightness and immediacy. But you can't really go back and change it once it is made. Clay, on the other hand, is a bit more like an oil painting. You can work on it for a longer time; and it has a more fluid look. The two methods do look quite distinct, even if you were creating a similar pattern.

Do you see your work as an art form?
Oh yes, absolutely. I think you have to be a bit of a guerilla artist. Somebody is buying your decoration; so there are lots of layers involved in creating something, layers of meaning, really. And that's in the design.

What could that be?
I am very conscious of the underlying geometry of a ceiling. And the successful use of modeling—whether it is stucco or in clay—is using the traditional shapes in a new way, extending the range of possible shapes.

Does your experience as a sculptor help you visualize what a design on paper will look like in 3D?
Yes, for the sculptor, even the clay itself is like a drawing material. While one sketches out a complete design, it is much more advantageous to work out the detail that you want in the clay. It comes out of a feeling in your hands in a completely different way than is possible with a drawing. The final cast might actually look very distinct from the drawing.

And how is that with stucco then?
With stucco, you only have a short window of working time, about four to six hours. So you must be very certain of what you are going to do. Sometimes you can work freehand, if you know very clearly the part of the design you want to do. But often I work out the design first in clay and then copy it in stucco, especially when I am doing something complex in stucco.

Do you feel like ceilings are missing something in modern architecture?
When I see a ceiling with nothing on it except light fittings, it feels to me like it is really missing something. Once I asked a client who was commissioning wall panels, "Weren't you interested in commissioning a ceiling?" Their reply: "No, because we never look up." But that, respectfully, is not right. We don't look up anymore, because there is nothing to look up to and at. When there is a decorative ceiling, you will look at it, and you will look at it again and again. Clients say to us, "I noticed this detail the other day, and I never noticed it before." They were sitting in the room and looking up, and suddenly a different perspective presented itself. And that's the way it should be.

Colorful Minimalism

Founded in 2014, Crosby Studios has made a splash on the interiors scene, engaging in sophisticated play with sculptural lines, contrasting textures, and surprising colors. Working between New York and Moscow, co-founder Harry Nuriev cites among his influences Le Corbusier and Chanel, the Russian avant-garde, and modern Japanese architects. His spaces fuse high and low, old and new, where raw concrete walls dialog with the warmth of wood, smooth arches, and sleek furnishings. Several projects plumb the potential of the color pink to both harmonize and accentuate. Pink screed flooring brings levity to a monochrome palette and patches areas where original floorboards were damaged. A furniture series combines the refinement of classic architecture with precision engineering and minimalist proportions for the perfect balance of functionality and beauty. For Nuriev, "Quality is like a human being. Everything is in its place: nails, ears, eyebrows. Everything is necessary, functional, and very beautiful. 'No' or 'impossible' should be avoided." ✗

Left, a beauty parlor fuses minimalism with contrasts in texture. Above, Crosby Studios' furniture collection in brass and powder-coated steel. Right, Gleaming brass reflects a brash sense of industrial chic.

Classic with a Modern Twist

Tassels, tie-backs, fringes, braids—these are some of the things used in passementerie, the art of making elaborate trimmings to embellish interior upholstery. This field of textile ornamentation was nurtured in France, where the Guild of Passementiers was established in the sixteenth century. Parisian company Houlès has succeeded in carrying this artisanal tradition into the twenty-first century by bridging traditional French and contemporary styles in its array of offerings. The family-run business was founded in 1928 by Félix and his son André Houlès in the garment district of Paris. Today, overseen by its president Philippe Houlès, the company is a leading designer and maker of high-end trimmings, decorative fabrics, and related hardware, with showrooms in Paris, Dubai, New York, and London. Headquartered outside of Paris in Noisy-sur-École, the company's production and logistics center is in Saint-Etienne in eastern central France—the historic birthplace of the French trimmings and ribbons industries. ✕

Trimmings—on everything from cushions to curtains—are making a comeback, lending contemporary spaces a sense of refinement and flair.

DECORATIONS TEXTILES   Houlès

French passementerie (trimmings) company Houlès was founded in 1928 by Félix and his son André Houlès in the garment district of Paris.

Anna Karlin and her W chairs, an interpretation of a classic Windsor chair in which each leg and spoke is hand carved (this page).

The Multidisciplinary Designer

From sculptural furniture and interiors to jewelry, digital, and print, English designer Anna Karlin explores design in all its facets. After graduating from the Glasgow School of Art in 2006, the London native worked as a graphic designer and art director. When she moved to New York City in 2010, she shifted away from solely client-driven work, developing her first collection of functional objects in 2012. "Not having studied product design means training does not inhibit me, and I find it liberating to work out processes as you go," says Karlin. Her new Glyph ensemble sees lights and sculptures suspended off of a peg rack above a hand-carved bench. Glyph reflects her narrative approach to design, conveying a sense of intimacy and mystery at the same time. Collaborating with local artisans is essential to the designer's multifaceted work and her commitment to upholding the heritage of craft. "If we don't utilize the remarkable craftspeople we're surrounded with, their skills will eventually cease to exist," she says.

American Luminaries

New York-based designer Jason Miller founded lighting company Roll & Hill in 2010 to bring high-quality, local craftsmanship to a wider audience. Inspired by the many mid-sized design manufacturers in Europe, Miller decided to fill the void he saw in the United States between megabrands and tiny workshops, creating a company that "could harness the talents of independent designers, while offering a small-batch production model that's more often associated with boutique studios." Roll & Hill's creative collaborations have resulted in a dynamic range of unique lighting fixtures drawing on a rich materials palette that includes brass, bronze, leather, wood, hand-knotted rope, and mouth-blown glass. At the company headquarters in Brooklyn, each piece is hand-assembled and produced on demand, allowing it to be customized to a client's needs. "Quality, to me, is the humanity behind an object. If an object feels like its maker cared about it, then it feels like a quality object," says Miller. ✕

Jason Miller (above) produces lighting by young design studios like Ladies & Gentlemen (left) or Lukas Peet (opposite). The following pages shows Miller's own design on the left next to Bec Brittain's Seed lamp on the right.

Iacoli & McAllister

Lighting

Allied Maker
New York, United States
Artisan-crafted, highly engineered, sophisticated yet simple lighting design solutions, working with love in natural materials, such as brass, glass, and hardwoods.
___www.alliedmaker.com

Apparatus
New York, United States
Combines historical and cultural aspects with modern hand-finished designs, using sensual materials. Also offers furniture, objects.
___apparatusstudio.com

Astep
Copenhagen, Denmark
Combination of traditional Italian design and technology to create meaningful design objects, and re-editing iconic objects.
___astep.design

Atelier Areti
London, United Kingdom
Elegant modern lamps, working with European manufacturers, primarily in Germany. Also offers furniture.
___atelierareti.com

Atelier de Troupe
Los Angeles, United States
Unique contemporary lighting, realized to the highest level and finished by their in-house design team and craftsmen. Also offers furniture.
___atelierdetroupe.com

B.lux
Basque Country, Spain
Contemporary design lamps by designers such as Werner Aisslinger.
___grupoblux.com

Bolichwerke
Östringen-Odenheim, Germany
Inspirational and functional lighting technology, with modern to classic design and custom-built solutions.
___bolichwerke.de

Brokis
Horní Dubenky, Czech Republic
Traditional mouth-blown glass, combined with selected materials such as wood and hand-hewn metal, producing both functional and decorative lightning.
___brokis.cz

Colonel
Paris, France
Young designs as well as new versions of classical designs, collections, and custom-mades. Also offers furniture, accessories, textiles, rugs, and wallpaper.
___moncolonel.fr

CTO Lighting
London, United Kingdom
Modern luxury lighting symbolizing the elegance and excellence of British design manufacturing, using only the finest materials, and working

Ferréol Babin

with elite British craftsmen.
___ctolighting.co.uk

Delightful
Rio Tinto, Portugal
Bohemian retro lighting design in various styles—from mid-century to modern.
___delightfull.eu

Erco
Lüdenscheid, Germany
Architectural lighting using LED technology, developing lighting tools for indoor and outdoor applications.
___erco.com

Fabien Cappello
Mexico City, Mexico / London, United Kingdom
Use local resources and local manufacture, as well as industrial processes, to produce carefully crafted objects. Also offers furniture and objects.
___fabiencappello.com

Flos
Bovezzo, Italy
Wide range of sophisticated designs from leading product designers past and present.
___flos.com

Fontana Arte
Corsico, Italy
Timeless design pieces since 1932, from Castiglioni to Herkner.
___fontanaarte.com

Foscarini
Marcon, Italy
Experimental lighting manufacturing, with a research atelier.
___foscarini.com

Gibas
Amandola, Italy
Combination of technological innovation and artisan creativity to produce high-quality lighting.
___gibas.it

Home Studios
New York, United States
Modern and elegant interiors, furniture, and lighting.
___homestudios.nyc

Iacoli & McAllister
Seattle, United States
Playfully elegant furniture, lighting, and other product collections and limited editions.
___iacolimcallister.com

Jordi Canudas
Barcelona, Spain
Offers experimental lamps and light installations.
___jordicanudas.com

Jorge Penadés
Madrid, Spain
Experimental lighting made from reclaimed leather. Also offers mirrors, seating, and storage solutions.
___jorgepenades.com
pp. 164–167

Kalmar Werkstätten
Vienna, Austria
Lighting concepts ranging from classic chandeliers to contemporary decorative luminaires and functional lighting solutions.
___kalmarlighting.com

Kaschkasch
Cologne, Germany
Minimalist, functional lighting elements.
___kaschkasch.com

Lambert & Fils
Montréal, Canada
Offers exquisite lighting products, small range.
___lambertetfils.com

Lamptique
Berlin, Germany
Handcrafted Art Nouveau and Art Deco lighting.
___lamptique.de

Le Klint
Odense, Denmark
A wide range of classic and innovative lamps produced in collaboration with various Scandinavian designers.
___leklint.com

Marcin Rusak

Lee Broom
London, United Kingdom
Luxury lighting using classical styles with an ironic twist.
Also offers luxury furniture.
___leebroom.com

Leuchten Manufactur Wurzen
Wurzen, Germany
Traditional brass and stainless steel chandeliers, since 1862.
___lmw-wurzen.de

Lightmaker Studio
Toronto, Canada
Mid-century inspired lighting, made in brass, nickel, copper, polished steel, and hand-blown glass.
___lightmakerstudio.com

Lindsey Adelman
New York, United States
Industrial modular lighting systems that capture the ephemeral, fleeting beauty of nature.
Also offers concrete tiles, wallpapers, and more.
___lindseyadelman.com

Jorge Penadés

Louis Poulsen
Copenhagen, Denmark
Danish lighting design based on the "form follows function" principle.
Also offers concrete tiles, wallpapers, and more.
___louispoulsen.com

Marset
Badalona, Spain
Refined and innovative lighting fixtures.
___marset.com

Mawa
Michendorf, Germany
Specialized in the design and production of a variety of classic and modern style lamps and lighting solutions for private and public spaces.
___mawa-design.de

Michael Anastassiades
London, United Kingdom
Combines product, furniture, and environmental design to produce minimalist utilitarian lighting elements.
Also offers mirrors and glasses.
___michaelanastassiades.com

Midgard
Hamburg, Germany
Long-established industrial lamp design.
___midgard.com

Modular
Roeselare, Belgium
Bold designs and innovative technology in architectural lighting.
___supermodular.com

Parachilna
Barcelona, Spain
Decorative lighting created by metalsmiths, glass-blowers, ceramicists, and other skilled craftsmen.
___parachilna.eu

Petite Friture
Paris, France
Elegant and accessible objects created by young designers such as Constance Guisset.
___petitefriture.com

Remains
New York, United States
Artisanal made-to-order and custom lighting, mirrors, and candlesticks.
___remains.com

Rich Brilliant Willing
New York, United States
LED fixtures for hospitality, workplace, and residential projects.
___richbrilliantwilling.com

Roll & Hill
New York, United States
Collaborations with exciting independent designers to create beautiful and unique lighting fixtures.
___rollandhill.com
pp. 74–77

Servomuto
Milan, Italy
Individually handcrafted limited edition lamp shades with classic style or contemporary prints.
___servomuto.com

Workstead
New York, United States
Custom lighting design and lighting consulting.
Also offers custom cabinetry and furniture design.
___workstead.com

Zava
Cornuda, Italy
Metallic carpentry lighting that unites craftsmanship and avant-garde technology.
___zavaluce.it

Decorations Stone

Ditta Medici
Rome, Italy
Decorative marble and renovations of ancient Roman marbles.
___dittamedici.it

Fumagalli & Dossi
Milan, Italy
Specialized in laster casts in the old Italian tradition.
___fumagallidossi.com

Geoffrey Preston Sculpture & Design
Ide, United Kingdom
Offers architectural sculpturing and decorative plasterwork for traditional British interiors.
___www.geoffreypreston.co.uk
pp. 56–63

Lapicida
Harrogate, United Kingdom
Elegant, elaborate marble flooring, stone and ceramic tiles.
Also offers onyx and petrified wood objects, for example bathtubs.
___lapicida.com

Scarpelli Mosaici
Florence, Italy
Specialized in the production of traditional Florentine mosaics adorned with gems and stones.
___scarpellimosaici.it

Städtische Meisterschule für das Vergolderhandwerk München
Munich, Germany
Church painting and monument preservation.
___fsflt.musin.de/home/msv/msv.htm

Geoffrey Preston

Stuck Höck
Augsburg, Germany
Plastering and stucco works and restoration.
Also offers stucco marble, sgraffito, marmorino, staff, mold construction, and cast stucco.
___stuck-hoeck.de

Stuck Tümmers
Gelsenkirchen, Germany
Traditional handmade stucco elements.
___stuck-tuemmers.com

Stuck Werner
Hamburg, Germany
Specialised in cornice elements and decorative ornamental plastering.
Also offers molding, wall panels, sculptures.
___stuck-werner.de

Decorations Metal & Glass

Bonnemazou Cambus
Paris, France
Design of flashy, ultra-modern doorknob collections consisting of different modular elements handmade in their Parisian atelier.
___bonnemazou-cambus.fr
pp. 246–249

The Nanz Company
New York, United States
Fine custom hardware, such as handles, hinges, locks, and fittings, over 3000 modern and historic products.
Also offers yacht hardware.
___nanz.com
pp. 86–89

Lavinia hexagonal armchair and Inge sofa (this page). Marta Sala with the Megan table/lamp in brass and gold marble, Jean Louis screen in chrome and linen with Pilar Screen/table/lamp, and Alastair modular sofa (left page).

The Secret Soul of Useful Things

Launched in 2015, Marta Sala Éditions (MSE) in Milan is a line of furniture, objects, and lighting created in collaboration with leading architects and designers. The enterprise builds on years of experience gathered by founder Marta Sala as a design curator for the iconic furniture company Azucena. The company was co-founded in 1947 by her mother, Maria Teresa Tosi, together with her uncle Luigi Caccia Dominioni, and Ignazio Gardella, two of the country's most prominent modern architects. According to Sala, "When you are the heir of great histories it is important to add something new." For her first three collections, Sala found the ideal creative partners in Claudio Lazzarini and Carl Pickering. The Rome-based architects are not only known for their buildings but also for the bespoke furniture they design. Under mottos such as "The Secret Soul of Useful Things" and "The Rule of Detail," MSE's collections are produced locally in the Brianza area, north of Milan, marrying a strong sense of craftsmanship with a contemporary mindset reflected in clean lines, modular elements, and technologically advanced fabrics.

Clockwise from above left: Wanda modular armchair, Dudina armchair, Silla armchair and Ludovico rug. Luis paravent, Elisabeth sofa, and Mathus coffee table are standing on the Ludovico rug with waxed brass or copper accents (right page).

At their state-of-the-art factory in New York, Nanz employs computer technology as well as traditional techniques to produce decorative and functional hardware.

From Knob to Hinge

With a five-person studio at their New York City headquarters in SoHo and a state-of-the-art factory on nearby Long Island, The Nanz Company is dedicated to manufacturing fine custom hardware for residential and commercial projects, including handles, hinges, locks, and fittings. Founded in 1989 by Steve Nanz and Carl Sorenson, the company started out refurbishing historic hardware for home restoration projects, which led to developing their own line of brass reproductions with advanced engineering. Today, Nanz prides itself on handling every aspect of the design and fabrication of over 3,000 products in a wide array of designs and finishes, as well as creating custom solutions according to the highest standards in craftsmanship and sustainability. The quality of Nanz's products is reflected in subtleties of proportion, shape, and finish. "Things that are done by hand are the best, and a discerning eye can tell the difference. We like each of our products to make the viewer stop and appreciate what he or she beholds." ✕

To ensure highest quality, Nanz controls all aspects of manufacturing, from engineering, pattern making, casting, machining, chasing, plating, and finishing, to door-by-door packing and shipping.

Tailored Elegance

Fromental is a British wallcoverings atelier founded in 2005 by Tim Butcher and Lizzie Deshayes. Both studied textile design and worked in fashion, influences that are clearly felt in their repertoire of designs hand-painted or stitched onto paper and other textiles—most notably silk. "We pioneered the technique of embellishing wall coverings with fine silk embroidery, taking an already supreme decorative form to new heights of opulence," note the designers. Their silk, paper-backed wallpapers are designed in London and then made in Wuxi, the current center of China's silk industry. After being hand-painted, the silk is meticulously embroidered in nearby Suzhou, a city famous for its silk embroidery going back to the eighteenth century. Bridging classic and contemporary, Fromental's designs include modern interpretations of eighteenth-century chinoiserie as well as abstract and geometric patterns in monochromatic and vibrant colorways. According to Butcher, "For many years, wallpaper was not considered a 'big-ticket' item, but that has changed." ✕

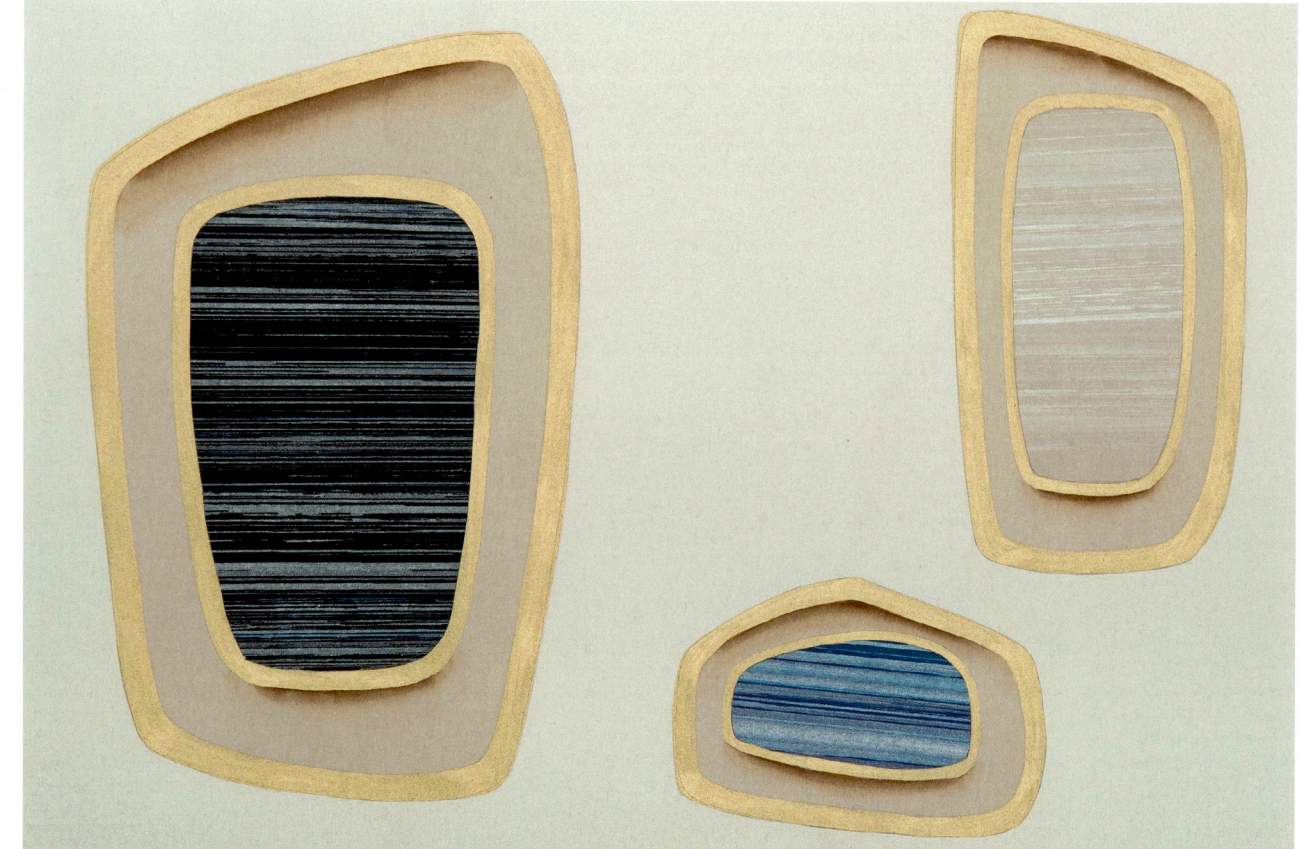

Roche Meteore pattern by Fromental using Roger Thomas sketches with faux gems set into a bold framework (right). An angular hand-painted tree contrasts with delicate embroidered cherry blossoms (below). Fromental's Caisson is a modern trompe l'oeil imitating coffered paneling (right page).

Reinterpreting Traditional Italian Craft

The Novecento Chair is based on the iconic Chiavari created in 1807 (left page). La Solferino, a modern reinterpretation of the Chiavari; instead of woven reeds this model uses modern paracord for the seat (above right).

With their product brand Eligo, Milan-based designers Alberto Nespoli and Domenico Rocca revive and reinterpret traditional Italian artisanal pieces through a modern lens. After studying interior architecture and design at Politecnico di Milano in 2007, the duo founded an interior design company in 2011, and Eligo in 2014. The name comes from the Latin word *eligere* meaning "to choose with care and elegance." This reflects the designers' approach to synthesizing aesthetics, ethics, passion, local culture, and Italian tradition. This comes to fruition in their collaborations with Italian artisans skilled in traditional techniques such as weaving, glassblowing, pewter casting, and ceramic decoration. The starting point for their Chiavari chair collection is the iconic lightweight Chiavarina chair, created in 1807 in the town of Chiavari by Gaetano "il Campanino" Descalzi. Eligo has since added further limited-run reinterpretations of historic models from the nineteenth and mid-twentieth centuries. ✗

Vintage Furniture

1st dibs
New York, United States
International online marketplace for design objects, antiques, and furniture, .
___1stdibs.com

Azucena
Milan, Italy
Italian design by Luigi Caccia Dominioni or Ignazio Gardella, manufactured by local artisans from Lombardy.
___azucena.it

Dorotheum
Vienna, Austria
Antique furniture auctions since 1707.
___dorotheum.com

Edition20
Munich, Germany
Online research platform for twentieth-century design classics.
___edition20.com

Frank Landau
Frankfurt am Main, Germany
Dealer for selected vintage design objects, fine art, and interior design.
___franklandau.com

Lauritz
Hamburg, Germany
Online auction house for antiques, accessories, clocks, and fashion.
___lauritz.com

Markanto
Cologne, Germany
Online marketplace for design classics by Knoll International, Vitra, or Zanotta.
___markanto.de

Nilufar
Milan, Italy
Gallery for mid-century gems and contemporary works, with a three-story design depot.
___nilufar.com

One Collection
Hamburg, Germany
Handmade design furniture from the first half of the twentieth century, working with manufactured pieces only from Scandinavian, Austrian, and Austro-American architects.
___wohnkultur66.de

Pamono
Berlin, Germany
Online marketplace for international vintage furniture and design objects, including a magazine.
___pamono.de

Quittenbaum
Munich, Germany
Auction house specialized in Art Nouveau, Art Deco, Murano glass, and modern art.
___quittenbaum.de

The Apartment
Copenhagen, Denmark
Show apartment with vintage furniture, mirrors, rugs, and lighting available for purchse.
___theapartment.dk

John Sankey

Bloc Studios

Re-editions

Carl Hansen
Gelsted, Denmark
Re-editions of Scandinavian mid-century furniture, from designers such as Hans J. Wegner, Ole Wanscher, Poul Kjaerholm, Mogens Lassen, adding a modern twist with contemporary fabrics and colors.
___carlhansen.com

ClassiCon
Munich, Germany
Re-editions of designs by Eileen Gray, Eckhart Muthesius, or Otto Blümel. Also offers contemporary designs by Sebastian Herkner or Victoria Wilmotte.
___classicon.com

Fritz Hansen
Allerød, Dänemark
Re-editions of Scandinavian mid-century furniture, from designers such as Arne Jacobsen and Bruno Mathsson. Also offers contemporary designs by Cecile Manz and GamFratesi, among others.
___fritzhansen.com

Gubi
Copenhagen, Denmark
Reinterpretations of furniture designs by mostly Scandinavian and French designers, such as Greta M. Grossman, Mathieu Matégot, Jacques Adnet, Kerstin H. Holmquist, and (Italian) Gio Ponti, adding a modern twist with contemporary fabrics and/or colors. Also offers contemporary designs by OeO Studio and Space Copenhagen, among others.
___gubi.com

Knoll
East Greenville, United States
Re-editions of design classics of the most famous designers of the last century, including Florence Knoll, Harry Bertoia, Marcel Breuer, Eero Saarinen, Mies van der Rohe, and Richard Schultz. Also offers contemporary furniture and accessories by designers such as Barber & Osgerby, Jehs+Laub, Piero Lissoni, and others.
___knoll.com

Molteni & C.
Giussano, Italy
Re-editions of furniture designs by Gio Ponti and Tobia Scarpa. Also offers contemporary designs by Foster & Partners, Vincent van Duysen, Luca Nichetto, and others.
___molteni.it

PP Møbler
Allerød, Denmark
Family-owned Danish joinery workshop exploring the possibilities of wood and producing re-editions of original designs by Hans J. Wegner and Jørgen Høj. Also offers contemporary furniture pieces by designers such as Zaha Hadid or, most recently, Thomas Alken.
___pp.dk

Tecta
Lauenförde, Germany
Re-editions of original (Bauhaus and earlier) designs by Marcel Breuer, Walter Gropius, El Lissitzky, Gerrit Rietveld, and Karl-Friedrich Schinkel. Also offers contemporary designs by Daniel Lorch, Andree Weißert, and others.
___tecta.de

Vitra
Weil am Rhein, Germany
Re-editions of design classics by Charles & Ray Eames, Jean Prouvé, George Nelson, Isamu Noguchi, and Alexander Girard. Also offers Vitra Campus, Design Museum, and contemporary productions of furniture and accessory pieces by designers such as Antonio Citterio or Hella Jongerius.
___vitra.com

VS (Neutra)
Tauberbischofsheim, Germany
Manufacturer of furniture by Austrian architect and designer Richard Neutra, in three different color and material series.
___neutra.vs.de

&tradition

Expressive and Organic

Based in Maastricht, where he graduated from the Academy of Fine Arts in 2009, German designer Valentin Loellmann combines wood and other materials to create furniture that feels atmospheric and organic. For his Seasons series of benches, tables, and stools, polished oak surfaces are subtly connected to legs made from charred and waxed hazel wood branches, left naturally uneven to retain a dynamic element. The joints are filled in with a mixture of sawdust and glue so that no sharp edges remain. In his Brass furniture series, charred black oak and walnut are fused with slender bronze frames. Instead of casting brass elements, Loellmann cut shapes out of brass plates as if working with fabric, then bent and welded them to form organic shapes whose polished surfaces are in constant play with light and reflection. "I treat my materials like living organisms," Loellmann says of his approach. "The pieces I make have always developed out of an interest in materials, their travels, and the histories they tell. Using craftsmanship techniques, I create new narratives with them."

Maastricht-based German designer Valentin Loellman has gained international acclaim for his subtly complex furniture that combines classic elements with organic forms.

The chairs are from the Brass series whose slender brass frames contrast with their soft wooden top (this page). Dining set from the fall/winter collection, charred hazelnut branches and oak (left page).

Kazumi Yoshida is a New York-based painter, sculptor, and the longtime art director of American fabrics and wallpaper company Clarence House.

A Colorful History

"I want students just starting out in design to understand how exciting fabrics can be, how they are just as glamorous as fashion," says Kazumi Yoshida, painter, sculptor, and the driving force behind Clarence House. The American company is famous for its hand screen printing of fabrics and wallpapers, high-style textures, hand-loomed brocades, and other exclusive textiles. Clarence House was co-founded by New York interior designer Robin Roberts, who started out in 1961 by importing European fabrics. Eventually, the style-setting firm became involved in every aspect of the creative process. Yoshida joined in 1981 as art director, having studied architecture in Japan and the U.K. before moving to New York in the 1970s. Today, he is still part of each design process, from the initial concept to the finished product. Many of the company's bold, whimsical designs originated in his studio as watercolor paintings. According to Yoshida, "We all need a little fantasy. We should all be inspired to play in creative ways."

DECORATIONS TEXTILES　　　Clarence House

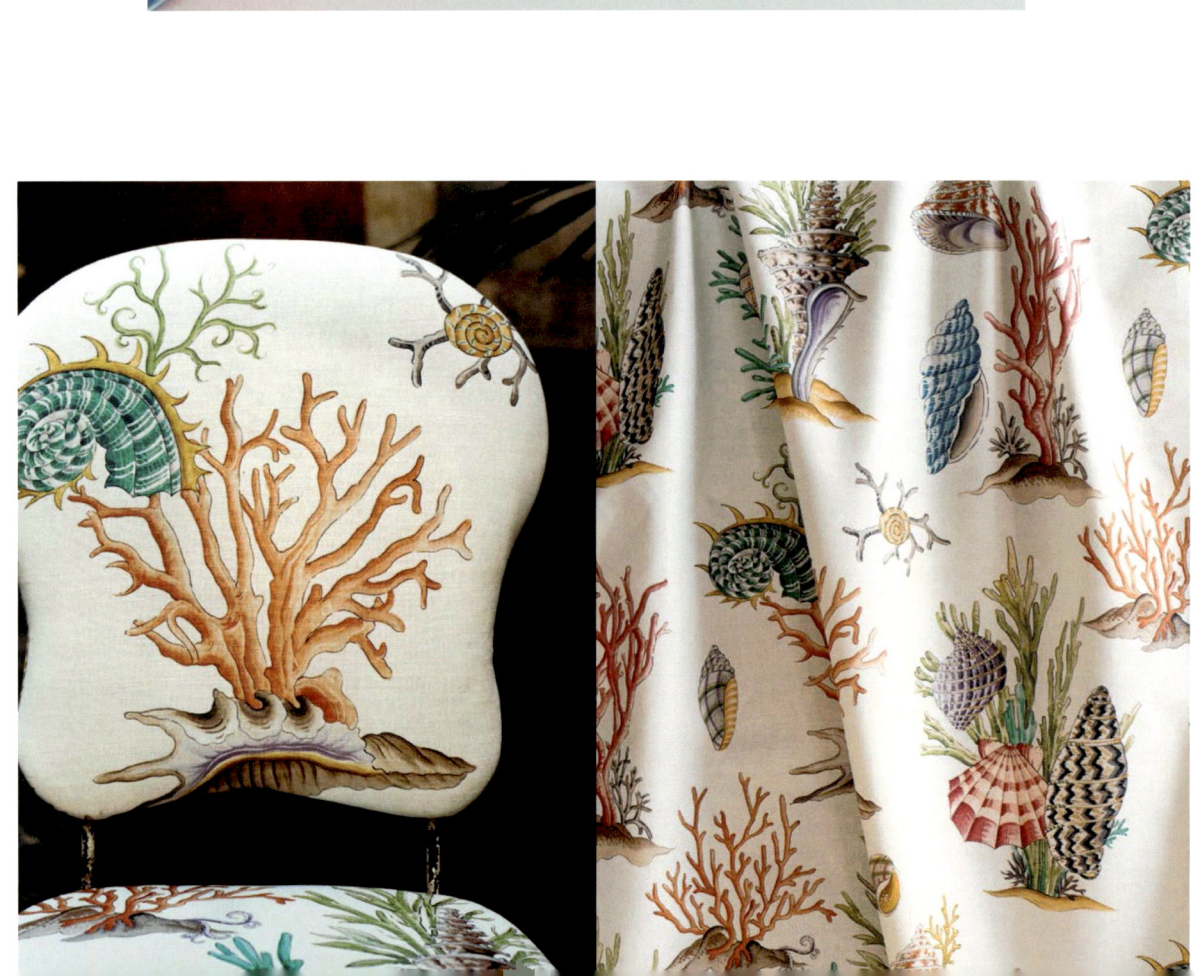

Many of the bold and whimsical patterns found on Clarence House luxurious hand screen-printed wallpapers and fabrics originated as watercolor paintings by Yoshida. Above, he paints a playful interior.

Soane Britain
Networking with the Past

A passion for preserving traditional British crafts led Lulu Lytle to co-found Soane Britain, creating a new market and appreciation for locally produced furniture, fabrics, and interiors.

Thanks to Lulu Lytle's (top) intervention, Britain's last rattan weavers in Leicestershire still create stunning pieces like The Ripple Console (left page).

Rattan in all its versatility: Used for a compact two-tier side table (this page), the airy Lacy mirror and the Daisy hanging light (right page).

These days transparency equals integrity: from food to fashion to furniture, knowing where and how the things we consume and live with are made helps us to make informed decisions. Which makers and production philosophies do we want to support? For Lulu Lytle, the co-founder and creative director of the London-based furnishing brand Soane, that transparency is sacred. Everything Soane produces is made in Britain by local craftsmen she knows personally. Founded in 1997, Lytle's company is built on an extensive network of manufacturers of furniture, fabrics, and wallpapers that evoke the charm of past centuries with their playful, romantic, and eccentric allure.

Designs from the past play an integral role at Soane. Have you always been fascinated by history?
Oh, always. I suspect it was fostered all through childhood, viewing house sales with my mother whenever there was one. And we always kept an eye out for an antique shop. Later, I moved to London to study Egyptology, and started going to Portobello Market every Saturday. That really cemented my fascination for craftsmanship. All the great experts were there, from people who specialized in continental silver to old maps, lithographs, and garden statuary—a complete breadth of disciplines of different manufacturers.

Do you think Portobello Road can still offer that today to a young, curious person?
Yes, definitely. Sadly it has diminished enormously since I started going. A lot of the great old arcades have been turned into miserable shopping arcades. But there are still some real experts there.

So after graduation, you started working for an antiques dealer?
Exactly, which was wonderful. I went to more auctions and spent time talking to many antiques dealers and restorers, realizing that, while antiques were a great interest of mine, I was really keen to learn more about making. So one summer, I went traveling around England, meeting lots and lots of different makers. I had plotted my journey on a map based on research I did in the Craft Council's library, where you can look up makers by discipline. I would spend different weeks in different areas, talking to makers, who were very generous with knowledge and connected me with other craftsmen. Everybody played a part in helping to shape my journey; and that's how I found the initial workers that I worked with.

How did this "tour de makers" lead to Soane?
Well, as with everything, luck was involved. The antiques dealer Christopher Hodsoll spoke to me, saying he owned some old designs which he had been making for a while. And I had new designs that I sketched. So putting these together made sense. Initially our aim was to show people that you can

make beautiful things with no concession to quality in England. I learned that the skills still existed despite the decimation of craft from the 1970s onwards, when so much had gone to the Far East.

Are your designs often based on antiques?
Yes. Many of our pieces are inspired by antique originals I've bought. What I am always drawn to, even more than extraordinary quality, is atmosphere. Pieces that have some evidence of human soul.

Do you think old pieces are more interesting because they can be a bit more playful?
This playfulness is very often in the detail. Personally, I have always been drawn to furniture inspired by animals. And particularly, fantastic Irish eighteenth-century tables with wonderful huge lion masks and paw feet. I feel there is a certain sort of poise and tension in really good early Irish furniture.

Has your way of designing changed over the years?
Today, I start designing with the material in mind, and then look at the design based on an increased knowledge of how that material will react. That's what has been really fascinating in the last 20 years, spending time in workshops and seeing the potential and limitations of every material, especially rattan.

Why rattan?
For many reasons. There is a romance to it that very few other materials have. It's an extraordinary material, stronger and more durable than most other plants. I discovered plant material for use in furniture when I was studying Egyptology. With Soane, it started with a fantastic sofa I wanted to copy that reputedly came from a Mountbatten house in Ireland. But when I searched for a weaver, everyone told me, "England no longer has a rattan industry." But eventually we found Angraves—the last makers who subsequently made all rattan furniture for us, until they closed Christmas 2010. But we took on their rattan weavers, and now it's our workshop; and we even established an apprenticeship scheme for it.

How did rattan find its way to Britian?
In the eighteenth and nineteenth centuries, trade with the Far East increased, and rattan was imported to Europe. People fell in love with its exoticism and versatility, first in continental Europe, but soon also in England. Germany and Austria had flourishing wicker industries in the nineteenth century; and in 1907, an enlightened social reformer named Harry Peach founded Dryad, the first British rattan manufacturer. Dryad has a very distinguished history: it contributed to the war effort by weaving shell cases and hot air balloon baskets, and also made rattan furniture for the Titanic.

Overall, do you want each design made by Soane to become an heirloom piece?
I certainly hope so. I really like to think that a Soane piece is a very long-term investment. That a client can say, my great-grandchildren will enjoy this. That's why it's so important that everything is made with absolute integrity. People, more than ever, need to trust the origin and authenticity of a piece.

Jan Hendzel

Furniture Wood & Natural Fibers

Aara Design
Harrow/Middlesex, United Kingdom
Solid wood furniture produced in India.
___aaradesign.co.uk

Anna Karlin
New York, United States
Contemporary furniture and lighting, some of them sculptural, made from wood and metal.
Also offers jewelry, interior design and set design
___annakarlin.com
pp. 72–73

Another Country
Dorset, United Kingdom
Contemporary craft furniture with atypical designs that call on the familiar and unpretentious forms of British Country kitchen style, Shaker, traditional Scandinavian, and Japanese woodwork. Also offers home accessories.
___anothercountry.com

Anton Doll Holzmanufaktur
Munich, Germany
Solid wood furniture, such as tables, chairs, and shelves in timeless designs.
___antondoll.de

Ateliers J&J
Brussels, Belgium
Limited edition furniture in metal frames made from locally sourced woods.
___ateliersjetj.com

BDDW
Philadelphia, United States
Exquisitely detailed furniture made from precious American woods.
Also offers ceramics.
___bddw.com

Branca
Lisbon, Portugal
High-quality handcrafted seating and storing units in cutting-edge design.
___branca-lisboa.com

Buchholz Berlin
Berlin, Germany
Design and production of individual tables made out of raw wood from regional forests and recycled wood waste.
___buchholzberlin.com

Casamania
Vidor, Italy
Furniture with a highly characteristic use of color and playful shapes.
Also offers lighting and home accessories.
___horm.it

Charles Dedman
Ropley, United Kingdom
Design and production of timber furniture using Craft-Tech, the updating of traditional

Lison de Caunes

processes with modern tooling.
___charlesdedman.co.uk
pp. 162–163

Dare Studio
Brighton, United Kingdom
Contemporary, straight-lined furniture and lighting products.
___darestudio.co.uk

De La Espada/Autoban
New York, USA/Istanbul, Turkey
Furniture and lighting that plays with reinterpreting the familiar through modern forms and contrasting materials.
___delaespada.com

Dedon
Lüneburg, Germany
Woven outdoor furniture by designers such as Jean-Marie Massaud.
___dedon.de

E15
Frankfurt, Germany
Innovative furniture, lighting, and accessories, sustainably and innovatively produced
___e15.com

Eligo Studio
Milan, Italy
Handmade traditional Italian furniture and accessories—from chairs to copper pots.
___eligostudio.it
pp. 94–95

Ercol
Princes Risborough, United Kingdom
Seating and storage units in Shaker style and contemporary designs by, for example, Lucian Ercolani.
___ercol.com

Fabian Fischer
Freiburg, Germany
Production of hand-carved wooden furniture, for example Windsor chairs.
___fabianfischerhandcrafts.com

Ferréol Babin
Dijon, France
Engineering design and furniture with artificual surface designs.
Also offers lighting.
___ferreolbabin.fr

Fred Ganim
Melbourne, Australia
High-end chairs, tables, and shelves in experimental forms.
___fredganim.com

Garnier & Linker
Paris, France
Combining contemporary design and rare materials such as Japanese washi paper or Kityama cedars.
___garnieretlinker.com
pp. 122–123

Gärsnäs
Gärsnäs, Sweden
Quality wooden and rattan furniture in Viennese netting.
___garsnas.se

GTV
Turin, Italy
Production of classic and contemporary seating, often in combination with traditional bentwood-pieces, in the style of the late nineteenth century.
Also offers stools, benches, accessories.
___gebruederthonetvienna.com

Higgs & Crick
Saffron Walden, United Kingdom
Highest quality mid-century lounge furniture, glassware, and accessories.
___higgsandcrick.com

Impagliando
Meda, Italy
Specialized in woven chairs, day beds, and accessories.
___impagliando.it

Jallu Ebénistes
Bazouges la Perouse, France
Creates museum-quality furniture, wall panels, and one-of-a-kind pieces, using straw marquetry, gypsum, mica, vellum/parchment, shagreen, precious wood veneers, and fine metal work.
___yannjallu.net

Ferréol Babin

david/nicolas

Jan Hendzel
London, United Kingdom
Design and production of original furniture formed from reclaimed timbers and English grown hardwoods.
___janhendzel.com

Javier S. Medina
Madrid, Spain
Unique mirrors and animal heads made from bamboo, wicker, rattan, and fibers.
___javiersmedina.com

Joseph Walsh
Cork, Ireland
One-off sculptural furniture pieces with collector's value.
___josephwalshstudio.com
pp. 252–255

Kraud
Karlsruhe/Munich, Germany
Artificial, experimental furniture, luminaires, and accessories in unique forms with a sculptural feel.
___kraud.de

Lison de Caunes
Paris, France
Straw marquetries made from dyed rye straw and inspired by Art Deco pieces.
___lisondecaunes.com
pp. 200–207

Ilot Ilov
Berlin, Germany
Design of experimental and playful both functional and emotional interiors and products.
___llotllov.de
pp. 230–233

Montana
Haarby, Denmark
High-end modular shelving systems in a variety of colors.
___montana.dk

Nicolas Aubagnac
Paris, France
Artful, elegant furniture such as cabinets with wooden inlays.
___nicolas-aubagnac.com

Oasiq
Antwerp, Belgium
Purposefully designed outdoor furniture with playful elements.
___oasiq.com

Objekte unserer Tage
Berlin, Germany
Young and minimalistic designs that blend craftsmanship, function, and form and include little eccentric details.
___objekteunserertage.com

Phloem Studio
Portland, United States
Timeless American furniture with an emphasis on natural materials and traditional joinery.
___phloemstudio.com

Piet Hein Eek
Eindhoven, Netherlands
Specialised in using scraps of wood to create distinctive furniture.
___pietheineek.nl

Sebastian Cox
London, United Kingdom

Kraud

Handmade timber furniture which brings coppiced timber into contemporary design.
___sebastiancox.co.uk
pp. 42–45

Skagerak
Aalborg, Denmark
Design and development of outdoor and indoor furniture, as well as wood flooring.
___skagerak.dk

Snickeriet
Stockholm, Sweden
Design and production of made-to-order and bespoke furniture and interiors.
___snickeriet.com

Soane
London, United Kingdom
Specialized in a big selection of rattan furniture. Also offers historical upholstery and metal furniture, lighting, fabrics, as well as wallpapers.
___soane.co.uk
pp. 108–113

Temper Studio
Wiltshire, United Kingdom
Kitchenware and furniture made from local English hardwoods.
___temperstudio.com

Thonet
Frankenberg, Germany
Chairs made from bent solid beech wood in Viennese netting. Also offers tubular steel furniture.
___thonet.de

Tom Fereday
Sydney, Australia
Exclusive one-off pieces as well as high-volume mass-produced objects—all with sustainable core practices.
___tomfereday.com

Vonnegut/Kraft

Unopiù
Milan, Italy
Luxurious outdoor design furniture for gardens, balconies, and terraces.
___unopiu.de

Valentin Loellmann
Maastricht, Netherlands
Artful wooden furniture in organic, almost anthroposophic shapes and warm colors.
___valentinloellmann.de
pp. 98–103

Zeitraum
Wolfratshausen, Germany
Sustainable hardwood furniture with clear minimalistic designs, made in Bavaria with traditional regional techniques.
___zeitraum-moebel.de

Garnier & Linker

Landscapes for Living

Ghent-based design studio Muller Van Severen came to be in 2011 when Fien Muller first decided to collaborate with her husband, Hannes Van Severen, for a gallery exhibition. Without any formal training in furniture design, they channeled their backgrounds in photography and sculpture into the creation of functional objects, producing a debut collection of multicolored tables, chairs, and shelves. The creative couple has since expanded their repertoire of what they describe as "landscapes for living." Bridging art and the everyday, they often incorporate varied functionalities into a single unit, such as sitting, storing, working, and relaxing. From the start, their materials have been strong and simple, using steel tubing, leather, or polyethylene panels. The latter is commonly used in the catering industry, explains Muller, where different colors are used for each particular food: yellow for poultry, blue for fish, and green for vegetables. "We used all the colors available of that material, but it's their combination that makes the pieces special." ✕

Edgy All-rounder: At Muller van Severen, sheets of leather and colourful polyethylene panels are suspended in steel frames, resulting in radically reduced, multifunctional furniture.

Artisanal Ventures with Ancient Materials

"For us, quality often rhymes with time. Taking time to choose the materials, the right production workshop, creating prototypes, and trying again if the result is not fully satisfying," explain Garnier & Linker. The Paris-based duo met during their studies in product design and interior architecture at the École Camondo in Paris. After working with studios such as India Mahdavi and Studio KO, they set out on their own in 2015. Uniting master craftsmanship with a joy for experimentation, Garnier & Linker design small-series furniture and lighting creations revealing the beauty and complexity of ancient materials such as alabaster, obsidian, bronze, plaster, and cast glass. For a recent furniture series, they traveled to the forests of northwestern Kyoto to source natural and charred Kitayama cedar. For more than 600 years, these trees have been carefully cultivated to produce tall straight trunks without knots, which reveal beneath their bark fragrant timber with a unique rippled texture. ✕

For their Kitayama furniture series, Guillaume Garnier (below right) and Florent Linker (below left) collaborated with craftsmen in the small village of Kitayama, Japan where the best cedar is grown for traditional Japanese architecture.

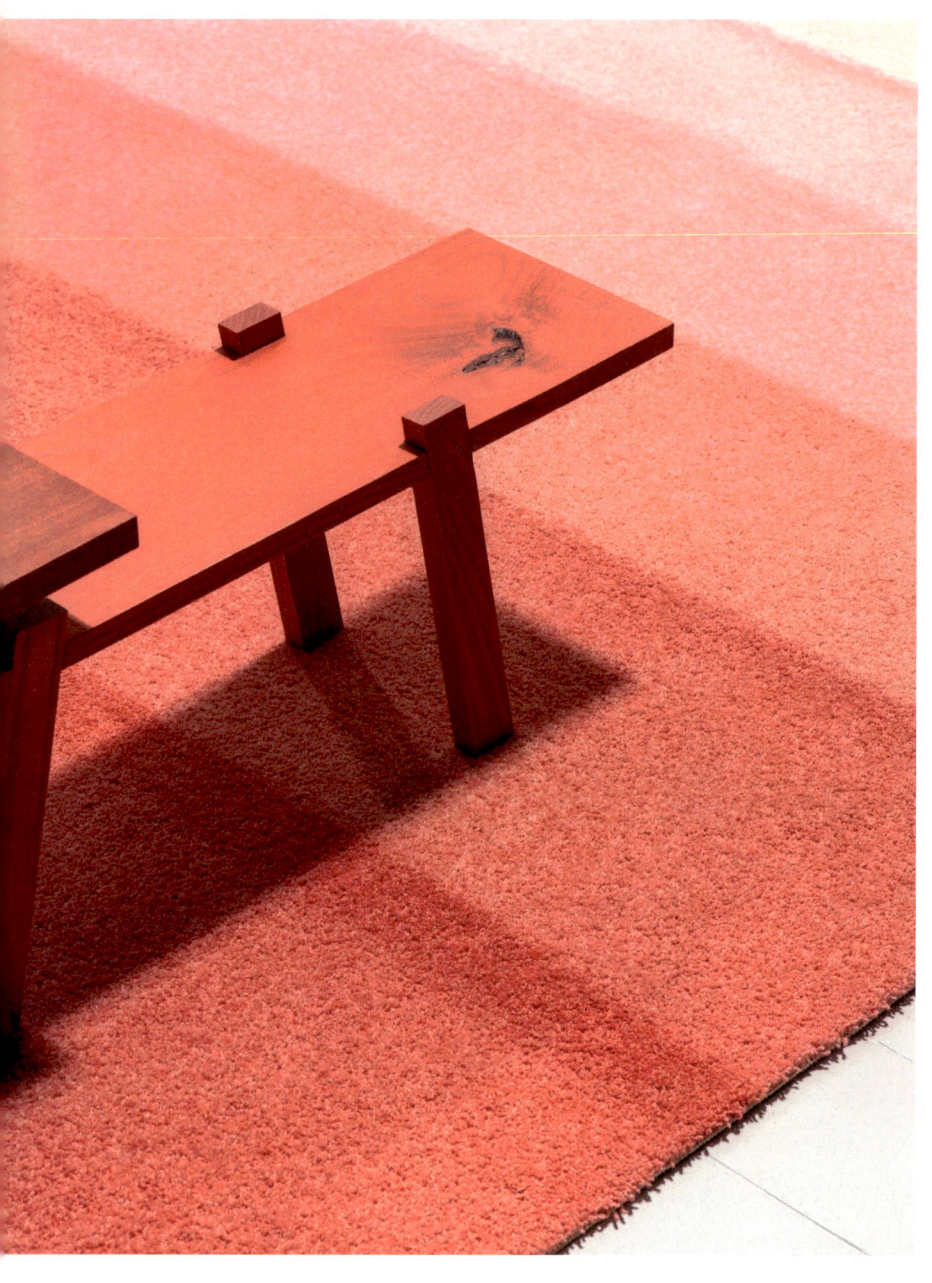

Reviving Retired Rugs in a Range of Red

Dutch design studio RENS revives the creative life of industrial leftovers in the form of new and unique products with Re-vive, their collaboration with global carpet firm Desso. Remnants from discontinued rug collections are submerged into red dye to create linear gradient designs, while the individual approach ensures that no two results are the same. The process achieves a vibrant layering effect as the original yarn colors blend with the red dye. "The color red makes a bold statement signaling to people that textile materials should not be wasted," explain the designers. Now nearing its 10th anniversary, RENS was born at the Academy of Art and Design St. Joost in Breda, where its founders, Renee Mennen and Stefanie van Keijsteren, both studied. The duo's creations are driven by their research into new materials and techniques: "For us, the beauty lies in the process and not only in the 'finished' product. Color and the behavior of material often play a key role in our designs." ✕

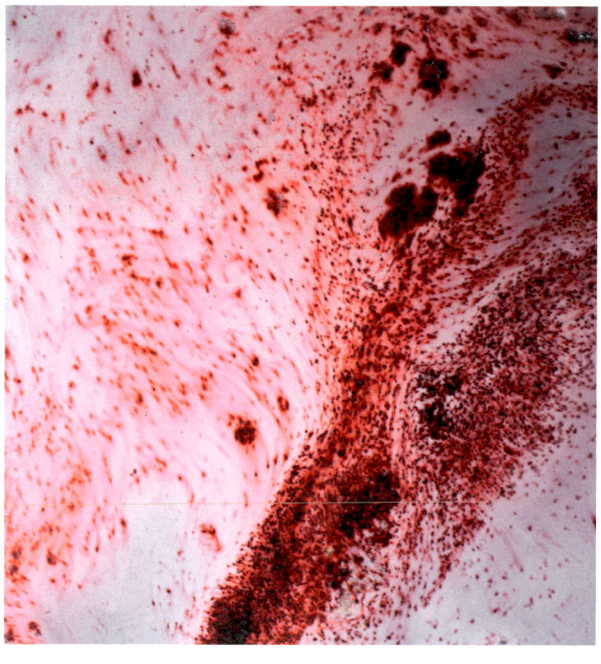

RENS revived retired Desso rugs by re-coloring them using red dye (this page). A similar technique is used by the Dutch designers for their upcycled clothing project Rood (right page).

Manually applied layers of red dye blend with the original color of the rug yarn to produce unique shades every time.

DWA Design Studio   FURNITURE STONE

DWA, in collaboration with Mariotti Fulget, explores the design potential of Silipol, an industrial alternative to marble developed in Italy after the Second World War.

Mid-Century Materialism

Frederik De Wachter and Alberto Artesani, who co-founded the Milan-based DWA design studio in 2005, have long been fascinated by the marble-like cladding used on Milan's first subway station walls in the 1960s. Called Silipol, it is a composite of granite powder, marble, and cement that is compressed into slabs. Introduced in the 1950s, it became a popular material for paving large surface areas. DWA embarked on a new creative journey when they came into contact with the Italian firm Mariotti Fulget S.r.l., which holds the patent for the new material. Since 2016, DWA has been exploring ways in which this industrial material can be "oriented towards a more intimate, accessible, and everyday dimension" through their collaborative Silipol Studies. Free of synthetic additives, Silipol is recyclable and highly customizable in terms of color and texture. "Because it is a material with natural ingredients, each slab is unique," notes DWA. "The production process is not completely controllable, which adds a certain poetic element." ✕

DWA's first Silipol project with a table, chairs, and "carpet" (left page). The Silipol archives holds over 12,000 original "recipes" of carefully calibrated colored components by Italian architects such as Franco Albini, Giò Ponti, and Renzo Piano (left).

A Crowning Finish

Jende Posamenten Manufaktur is one of the last of its kind in Germany, producing handmade upholstery trimmings according to traditional techniques on historic machines, some dating back to the nineteenth century. The workshop's illustrious history begins in 1884 with its founding by the Wagler family in Berlin, who had worked in trimmings since the sixteenth century. In 1910, they were appointed as the purveyor of passementerie to the royal Prussian court, and continued the business for three generations until 2006. A former employee took over the firm and relocated it to Forst (Lausitz), a city once known for its textile industry. In 2013, the languishing workshop was revived by its new owners, Diane and Christian Jende. Today, their small team weaves, knots, and stiches fine trimmings for interior decorators, restorers, set designers, historic palaces, and private clients. "It's a true craft. We do everything here just like it was done 100 years ago," says Diane Jende. "And it's tangible; you can see how the machine works, how the hands work. People appreciate that." ✕

Jende in Germany builds on its illustrious history as the official supplier of passementerie for the royal Prussian court in the early 1900s.

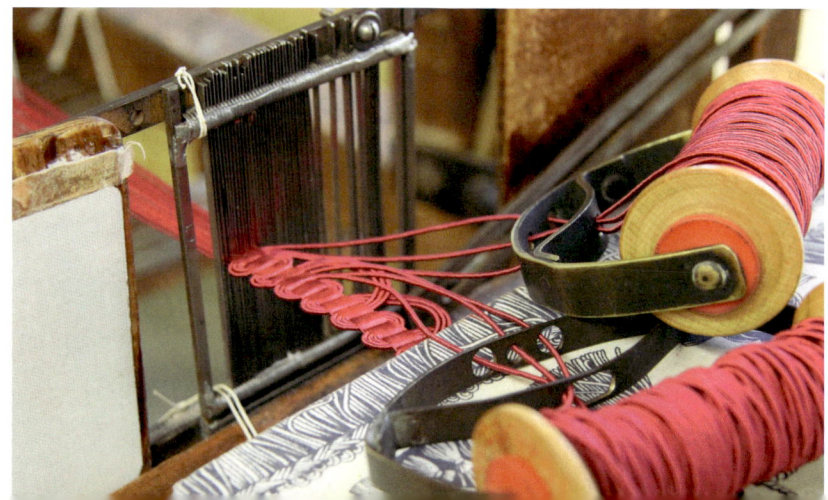

Jende Posamenten Manufaktur DECORATIONS TEXTILES 135

Tassels, fringes, braids, and tie-backs (on the left) are traditionally crafted and handmade in Brandenburg, Germany

The Quiet Beauty of Ceramics

Anchor Ceramics in Melbourne began as a side project for founder Bruce Rowe, who worked for several years in architecture after graduating with honors from the University of Western Australia in 2001. Curious to translate some of his drawings onto ceramic surfaces, he took a ceramics class in 2009 and was instantly taken with the immediacy and plasticity of one of the oldest and most basic human materials. "For me, ceramics is a kind of reconnection of the designer with the maker," says Rowe. Today the studio's small team produces ceramic tiles, lighting, outdoor and interior furniture, as well as sculptural objects, and collaborates with other small suppliers and workshops. Using a combination of traditional techniques and contemporary design strategies, their made-to-order tiles are handmade every step of the way, from rolling out the stoneware clay and cutting it into shapes to applying the custom glaze finishes developed within the studio. The tiles have refined textures and a distinct hand-formed aesthetic that creates subtle variations. ✕

The tiles are handmade by Anchor Ceramics, founded by Bruce Rowe in Melbourne. SCAPE are one-off ceramic forms sculpted by Rowe, each set is presented in a custom box (left).

Anchor Ceramics — DECORATIONS TILES — 139

SCAPE architectural forms are made using different Australian clays and Anchor's custom glazes (left page). The planters are thrown by hand on a potter's wheel (above and below). Handmade ceramic wall hooks (right).

FURNITURE UPHOLSTERY

Amy Somerville

New Beginnings and Old Passions

A lifelong passion for beautifully crafted furniture eventually led this native Pennsylvanian to design her own pieces.

FURNITURE UPHOLSTERY — Amy Somerville

C

The Yeti armchair in fluffy Mongolian sheepskin (right). Below, the Felidae II dining chair in yellow leather.

Career paths can be steady, straight climbs to the top, or they can move in twists and turns with sudden changes in direction, and with a completely different summit than the one initially set out for. Furniture designer Amy Somerville was working for a Swiss telecommunications giant as a user experience designer, but after moving to England and taking a bit of a break, she started her own furniture business. Growing up in Pennsylvania, surrounded by beautifully crafted antiques, she was looking for the same level of craftsmanship for her own range on the British Isles—and found it. Fusing Art Deco shapes with a British playfulness, Amy Somerville pieces show passion and joy in the details, and unparalleled quality in handmade, contemporary design.

What led you to start a furniture business?
I've always had an interest in antiques and furniture. I am Pennsylvania-Dutch and grew up in a region known for its outstanding furniture-making tradition. My father used to bring me along to house auctions of the Amish Mennonites who sell their homes and all the furniture they no longer want. He would volunteer to be the on-site lawyer simply because he loved the furniture. We spent our mornings walking around these auction sites with all these beautiful handmade pieces. Also, my grandfather took me to the antique markets.

WHEN YOU FIRST SIT ON A SOFA, IT SHOULD BE QUITE TIGHT-FEELING, AS IT WILL SOON LOOSEN UP LIKE A NEW PAIR OF SHOES.

Beautiful curves: the Casino Carver in Ruby Smoking Room Velvet with black ebonized satin legs and French natural nailing.

Leather skins waiting to be upholstered (left). Each of the decorative domed nails of the Babo Bench (right) is lined up and hammered in by hand.

that creative thinking to another business. With the move to London, I was looking for furniture pieces for my own home and found people who could make them for me. That was the start.

Was it a lengthy process to find the right craftsmen to work with?
Luckily, I met great people from the very beginning. The truth is that there are only so many people that have a craft ability. After I found one workshop for fitting out my apartment, I heard about others through the grapevine. It's a small industry here in the U.K.—people know who can do what. And so far, I haven't stopped working with anyone; we share a mutual respect. I absolutely appreciate and admire what they do, knowing I can't do it. And they like our designs. We are dedicated to each other.

What were your first products?
We did a small collection, some of our best pieces I would say, like the Minx sofa and two curiosity cabinets. The idea behind it was to create a lounge for Greta Garbo. A masculine lounge but for a modern woman. Everything had this 1930s-influenced masculine-feminine contrast which actually hasn't changed that much.

What do you like about that era?
In terms of furniture development, it was a very exciting time. There was a whole turn toward modernism beginning in the 1880s. People tended to be more experimental and loose, a post-Victorian

So you inherited the passion?
Indeed. When I was living in New York, I was accused of owning a furniture petting zoo because I collected all sorts of beautiful things I didn't need. I feel that creative mindsets work in parallel. So if you work in one creative field—even if it's in the user experience research and development department of Swisscom, as I did—you can transfer

A PIECE OF FURNITURE SHOULD BE COMFORTABLE AND MAKE YOU HAPPY. IT'S AS SIMPLE AS THAT.

idealism showing with the Wiener Werkstätte, or Frank Lloyd Wright at the turn of the century.

You are passionate about using traditional production methods. Are they part of the whole manufacturing process?
At the beginning of the production of most products, we usually rely on some machinery. But toward the end, all of our pieces are assembled and finished by hand. With cast metal, for example, it's a mix of automated and manual work. Sometimes the bronze is cast; in other cases, a CNC machine carves a handle directly from a bar. Or think of wood veneer, for which you need a completely different skill set, fusing machine and manual work. The veneers are hand-placed into a spiral to be cut by a laser and then get hand-pieced together again.

How can one test the quality of a furniture piece?
If it's upholstery, you should find it phenomenally comfortable to sit in. But not so comfortable that it's squishy, because the materials break down over time. That's why, when you first sit on a sofa, it should be quite tight-feeling, as it will soon loosen up like a new pair of shoes. Upholstery prototyping is the most difficult—comfort can be such a challenge. The pieces have to wrap around your body and fit several different body types. You need to find the right balance for the rake and the curves. I like to compare it to sitting in a car and adjusting the seat.

How is it with wooden furniture?
With a desk, check if the drawers are dovetailed or glued. For a cabinet, a good thing to inspect is the door hinges. Personally, I try to design them with traditional hinges, bullet catches, and brass fixtures, so it feels fantastic when you close the doors. Some cabinetmakers like to use blum hinges because they are adjustable. But good cabinet making doesn't need adjustment. As long as you're not bringing it from a very humid environment into a dry environment, or vice versa, its wood shouldn't move very much. Overall, I would say, pay attention to how something is finished just as you would with a piece of clothing. A piece of furniture should be comfortable and make you happy. It's as simple as that.

Step by step: Solid wooden frames build the core of the stools (left) that will later be upholstered in rich fabrics in the workshop (above).

&tradition

Furniture Upholstery

&tradition
Copenhagen, Denmark
Modern Scandinavian furniture from iconic designers like Arne Jacobsen, as well as from contemporary designers, such as Jaime Hayon and the Norm Architects. Also offers tables and lighting.
___andtradition.com

Amy Somerville
London, United Kingdom
Handmade furniture, inspired by the Art Deco period.
Also offers tables and cabinets.
___amysomerville.com
pp. 140–147

Arflex
Giussano, Italy
Modern upholstery designs from minimalistic to entertaining, including re-editions of classic designs from Cini Boeri, Franco Albini, and Marco Zanuso. Also offers a selection of beds, poufs, chairs, and tables.
___arflex.it

B&B Italia
Novedrate, Italy
Minimalistic modern Italian sofas, armchairs, and chaise longues.
Also offers tables, executive office furniture, beds, benches, and storage solutions.
___bebitalia.com

Baxter
Como, Italy
Modern upholstery designs with a focus on high-end leather covering.
Also offers beds, chairs, tables, and lighting.
___baxter.it

BD Barcelona
Barcelona, Spain
Flamboyant modern seating with flashy details, by contemporary designers such as Jaime Hayon.
Also offers tables, storage, and accessories, with original designs by Dalí and Gaudí.
___bdbarcelona.com

Blå Station
Åhus, Sweden
Modern playful seating furniture, from opulent upholstery to wood and metal designs.
Also offers tables and outdoor furniture.
___blastation.com

Bolia
Aarhus, Denmark
Democratic, minimalistic modern Scandinavian seating furniture such as sofas or stools. Also offers tables, cushions, and other accessories.
___bolia.com

COR
Rheda-Wiedenbrück, Germany
Reduced high-quality furniture, including sofas, sofa beds, and chairs.
Also offers bar stools and benches.
___cor.de

&tradition

De Sede
Klingnau, Switzerland
Unique leather products, including sofas, loungers, and chairs. Also offers tables.
___desede.ch

Edra
Pisa, Italy
Edgy and playful seating furniture with eclectic covering in contemporary Italian design. Also offers beds, tables, and shelvings.
___edra.com

Francis Sultana
London, United Kingdom
Interiors and furniture favoring the opulent style of the 1920s and 1930s. Also offers interior design, lighting, accessories, limited editions, and bespoke pieces.
___francissultana.com

George Smith
London, United Kingdom
Classic and elegant handcrafted British-style upholstery , such as sofas and armchairs, in a range of fabrics and leathers. Also offers outdoor furniture, customized pieces, and designer collections by Jean-Louis Deniot, among others.
___georgesmith.com

Honoré
Marseille, France
Upholstered sofas and armchairs, mostly framed in metal, bringing in a touch of Hollywood Regency. Also offers tables, lighting, mirrors.
___honoredeco.com

John Sankey
Long Eaton, United Kingdom
Unique sofas, chairs, and foots stools made from leathers, velvets, flat weaves, and romantic florals from around the world.
___johnsankey.co.uk
pp. 208–211

La Chance
Paris, France
Paris-based design company, working with designers such as Luca Nichetto or Noé Duchaufour-Lawrence, producing furniture, lighting, accessories, rugs, and wallpaper with a strong and distinctive style.
___lachance.paris

Ligne Roset
Briord, France
Contemporary sofas and armchairs by designers such as Pierre Charpin or Inga Sempé.
___ligne-roset.com

Marta Sala Éditions
Milan, Italy
High-end and handmade furniture, such as upholstered seating, screens, desks, and other objects, designed by renowned architects like Lazzerini and Pickering. Also offers screens, desks, rugs, and lighting.
___martasalaeditions.it
pp. 82–85

Michael Felix
Los Angeles, United States
Specialised in upholstered sofas, benches, and armchairs, mostly covered in rich leather fabrics.
___michaelfelix.com

Minotti
Meda, Italy
Handcrafted, high-end furniture in modern yet timeless shapes, from stools to large sofas. Also offers tables, storage solutions, beds and linen.
___minotti.com

Molteni & C
Giussano, Italy
Timeless contemporary furniture with an emphasis on natural materials and traditional joinery, re-editions by Gio Ponti, new designs by Vincent van Duysen, Ron Gilad, and others. Also offers a whole range of furniture, from tables to storing solutions.
___molteni.it

Moroso
Cavalicco, Italy
Luxury sofas and seating in playful young designs. Also offers outdoor furniture.
___moroso.it

Marta Sala

Amy Somerville

Phelippeau Tapissier
Paris, France
Traditional and historic seating furniture from French Baroque to contemporary interpretations.
Also offers passements, tapestries, and window decor.
___phelippeautapissier.com

Poliform
Inverigo, Italy
Clean modern seating furniture by designers such as Jean-Marie Massaud and Rodolfo Dordoni.
___poliform.it

Poltrona Frau
Tolentino, Italy
Elegant Italian-made products, including sofas and chairs. Also offers tables, beds, and office furniture.
___poltronafrau.com

Promemoria
Valmadrera, Italy
Opulent upholstered furniture from sofa to pouf, influenced by Art Deco and Far Eastern cultures, handmade in Italy.
Also offers beds, writing desks, tables, mirrors, screens, and lamps.
___promemoria.com

Sancal
Murcia, Spain
Playful contemporary seating by young design studios like Note.
Also offers tables and sofa beds.
___sancal.com

Sé
London, United Kingdom
Highly-crafted and beautifully finished feminine objects, made of the finest, noblest materials by various designers, for example Nika Zupanc.
___se-collections.com

The Sitting Place
Stockport, United Kingdom
Antique upholstered furniture.
___thesittingplace.co.uk

Zanotta
Nova Milanese, Italy
Classic seating furniture by Carlo Molino, as well as contemporary designs, for example, by Noé Duchaufour-Lawrence.
Also offers beds, tables, and accessories.
___zanotta.it

Furniture Beds

And so to bed
Dorset, United Kingdom
Traditional bed design, inspired by historical originals, from Baroque to Gothic to Victorian.
Also offers fitting mattresses, additional bedroom furniture, lamps, throws, bed linen, and pillows.
___andsotobed.co.uk

Auping
Cologne, Germany
Minimalistic modern bed design. Boxspring beds with matching elements, such as coil spring mattresses and toppers.
___auping.com

Cantori
Camerano, Italy
Flamboyant modern bed designs with opulent, flashy bed heads.
Also offers a whole range of furniture, from tables to mirrors and seating, including armchairs and divans.
___cantori.it

Chelsea Textiles
London, United Kingdom
Traditional, historical bed designs with Swedish Gustavian flair or in French Country style.
Also offers a whole range of furniture, from nightstand, mirrors, tables, and seating, as well as textiles.
___chelseatextiles.com

Ege Textilmanufaktur
Ulm, Germany
Textiles such as bed linen, table cloth, lace, and embroideries but also down fillings.
___ege-manufaktur.de

Emmanuelle Simon

Bartmann Berlin

Hästens
Köping, Sweden
High-end minimalistic boxspring beds with all-natural components such as horsehair fillings, covered in their famous check pattern.
___**hastens.com**

Ironbed
Maintal, Germany
Metal and iron beds in traditional British shapes.
Also offers beds for the elderly, nightstands, and sofas.
___**ironbed.de**

LinenMe
Woking, United Kingdom
Bed linen, table cloths, kitchen and bathroom textiles, plaids, and drapes—all made from linen.
Also offers a small range of fashion.
___**linenme.de**

Luiz
Hürth, Germany
Handmade and natural customized bed linen and home couture in over 570 colors, Also offers table and bathroom linen.
___**luiz.com**

Muun
Berlin, Germany
Washable cold foam mattresses with a flippable core for four different grades of firmness that can be manufactured individually for two sleepers.
Also offers a minimalistic bed frame, pillows, duvet and small collaborations.
___**muun.co**

Savoir Beds
London, United Kingdom
High-end beds since 1905, from modern eye catchers to traditional beds, including horsehair mattresses, toppers and boxspring frames.
Also offers a range of dog beds and designer collections.
___**savoirbeds.de**
pp. 178–183

Schramm
Winnweiler, Germany
High-end modern boxspring beds with pocket spring mattresses, using all-natural components, such as horsehair fillings and cashmere.
Also offers designer collections and bathroom couture.
___**schrammwerkstaetten.de**

Simon Horn
Buriton, United Kingdom
Classic eighteenth- and nineteenth-century French beds, based on antique forms, but re-sized and handmade for modern living.
Also offers mattresses, bedroom furniture, and linen.
___**simonhorn.com**

Society Limonta
Costamasnaga, Italy
Handmade bed linen and home couture made of natural materials, such as linen, cotton, silk, wool, and cashmere.
Also offers table and bathroom linen.
___**societylimonta.com**

Treca
Paris, France
High-end modern boxspring beds with pocket spring mattresses, made with all-natural components, such as horsehair fillings and cashmere.
Also offers motor-adjustable beds, bedroom furniture, and designer collections.
___**treca-interiors-paris.com**

White & Soft
New York, United States
Handmade beds with all-natural materials such as horsehair, cotton, wool, and springs, made in Germany.
___**whiteandsoft.com**

Wittmann
Etsdorf, Austria
Specialized in high-end, handmade beds that can be customized in a modular system.
Also offers designer collections and furniture, from tables to seating to nightstands.
___**wittmann.at**

Tadeáš Podracký designs and produces high-end crystalware in the Czech Republic. Towers (on the right) won the Ludwig Moser Award, and has been produced by this glass manufacturer ever since.

Glass Whisperer

Born in 1989 in the Czech Republic, Tadeáš Podracký works at the juncture of art and industrial design, cultivating a creative approach based on comprehensive historical and material research. Studying fine and applied arts at the Academy of Arts, Architecture, and Design in Prague and at New York's School of Visual Arts, he graduated in 2014. Early on in his young career, his extensive and innovative work with glass earned him the moniker "glass whisperer." Building on his knowledge of the Czech glassmaking tradition by studying techniques from around the world, he draws inspiration from China, the United States, and Finland, among others. With a passion for experimentation, Podracký has recently broadened the scope of his work to explore other mediums, materials, and scales. He says that his work is driven by a continual search to answer the questions, "What drives individuals to create art, design, or architecture? What role does human instinct play and what are just cultural expectations?" ✕

Garde Hvalsøe's kitchen for Danish star chef Rene Redzepi is made of oak with raw steel and burnished brass fixtures (right). Søren Garde's own kitchen, made of Dinesen HeartOak (see pp. 18–27) with linoleum-clad cabinets and a steel countertop (right page).

New Danish Classics

Founded in 1993 by Søren Hvalsøe Garde, the almost eponymous company is known for its exclusive handcrafted kitchens, bathrooms, and other bespoke furniture. Behind Garde Hvalsøe are three cabinet makers and an architect united by a profound love of wood and pride in the Nordic design tradition. "We use wood to sit on, to sit at, to eat from, and for countless other purposes. Therefore, putting a beautiful wooden surface in your kitchen is a very natural choice," notes partner Søren Lundh Aagaard. Their products stand out with a sophisticated dialogue between raw and refined; wood such as maple, elm, and oak is combined with materials like steel, granite, or linoleum to achieve contrast and beauty. For Garde Hvalsøe, quality is defined by the use of good materials, local production, and pure, honest design. According to the team, "Our aim is to achieve the highest possible level of both aesthetics and functionality by the absence of unnecessary details." ✕

Garde Hvalsøe's kitchen collaboration with Copenhagen-based designers OEO studio is made of oak, raw steel, and marble.

Antea Brugnoni (left) and Marco Kinloch (below) surrounded by Kinloch's hand-painted designs blending old-world and contemporary charm.

An Imaginary Idyll

Delicately drawn figures invoking faraway lands, intricate foliage, and decorative patterns—the stuff of fairytales—drive the colorful collections of Roi du Lac. Based in Rome, the home decor brand was founded by Marco Kinloch and Antea Brugnoni in 2016. The brand's name, French for "king of the lake," is inspired by Kinloch's Scottish surname. Kinloch, who also has an eponymous luxury brand of hand-painted Italian silk scarves and ties, has his dreamy, hand-drawn illustrations printed on paper, fabrics, and ceramics. Produced in Italy, the charming collections feature on wallpaper, tablecloths, plates, candles, scarves, loungewear, and more. "It gives people an opportunity to choose who they are within my world," says Kinloch. His Scottish-Italian heritage and Brugnoni's worldly upbringing in Malaysia, Morocco, the Middle East, and Sicily help inform the brand's aesthetics, through which they "envisage designs and styles based on ideas from all parts of the world, both present and past."

Roi du Lac's patterns include reinterpretations of classical chinoiserie, fantastical creatures, and elements of western decorative art, used on everything from wallpaper and tabletops to scarves and ready-to-wear.

Charles Dedman's Zapotec furniture range is hand-built from walnut wood and then finished with laser-cut, Aztec-inspired marquetry.

Craft Meets Tech

Launching his studio in 2014 after studying product and furniture design at Kingston University London, Charles Dedman set out to make "contemporary, honest furniture that takes an evolutionary rather than revolutionary approach, refining the form and function rather than trying to redefine a product." He calls this hybrid approach Craft-Tech—updating traditional joinery processes with modern tooling such as computer-aided design. His Zapotec collection includes a sideboard, cabinet, and frames that are hand-built from walnut wood and finished with laser-cut marquetry; the collection is inspired by colorful Aztec patterns on Mexican rugs. Once the wood veneers are cut to 0.01 mm accuracy, they are assembled, pressed, and finished with traditional processes. The range can thus be made quicker and more accurately, Dedman notes: "Possibilities for large detailed designs are greater and can be produced in a financially viable manner. The craft moves into the market of batch customization." ✕

Leathering Lights

While many designers develop products based on the advantages of a material, Madrid-based Jorge Penadés started out by considering the disadvantages. After learning of the vast amount of leather discarded during the production of shoes, clothing, accessories, and upholstery, he set out to find a way to close the loop on waste. For his thesis in experimental design at the European Institute of Design (IED) in Madrid, he devised a production method that transforms leftover leather into an innovative material with new properties and application possibilities. The leather is shredded into strips and then mixed with a natural glue created by boiling down animal bones. "I decided that was the perfect option because bones and skins are both byproducts of the meat industry," says Penadés. The mix is then pressed into shapes and finished with shellac, a natural resin derived from insects. The resulting material, which he calls Structural Skin, can be cut and sanded like wood, then reheated and reshaped into new products for a zero waste, circular production process.

For his Structural Skin, Penadés was inspired by traditional Japanese Boro textiles, which unite the principles of mottainnai, an aversion to waste with boroboro, the appreciation of well-worn objects.

Structural Skin is hand made using natural materials: shredded leather is mixed with bone glue, then pressed into shapes and finished with insect-derived shellac (left page). The resulting building blocks are used for lamps, tables, and more.

Above: From sketch to finished product, on handmade ceramic biscuit plates.
Right: Costanza Paravicini at work.

Workshop-to-table

Since the early 1990s, Laboratorio Paravicini in Milan has been dedicated to the creation of exclusive handcrafted ceramic plates, made to order with bespoke designs or in limited series. According to the designers, "Our purpose was to create plates that could bring back to everyday tables the atmosphere and warmth that was lost to the industrial porcelain production." Upholding the Italian ceramic craft tradition, while reinterpreting it for the contemporary urban table, the workshop produces its own thin, white ceramic biscuit, on which artisan Costanza Paravicini and her daughter Benedetta Medici hand-paint or apply screen-printed or digitally printed designs. The final glazing is then applied over the decorations at a high temperature, producing a plate that is suitable for everyday use, indelible, non-toxic, and dishwasher safe. In some cases, the decoration is obtained by pressing a dry stamp onto the biscuit while it is still soft. The glazing then fills into the profile, creating delicate chiaroscuro effects.

Laboratorio Paravicini

Tableware

2016/
Arita, Japan/Amsterdam, Netherlands
Handmade ceramic objects made in Japan and in collaborations with international design talents such as Stefan Diez or Scholten & Baijings.
___2016arita.com

Anchor Ceramics
Melbourne, Australia
Modern and minimalistic ceramic objects, lighting, and tiles. Also offers one-off sculptures.
___anchorceramics.com
pp. 136–139

Artěl
Prague, Czech Republic
Luxury Bohemian crystal glassware pro-ducts with simple patterns and detailed depictions of flora and fauna.
___artelglass.com

Bitossi
Firenze, Italia
Simple and elegant tableware, combining ceramic material, glass, wood, and new materials.
___bitossihome.it

Bon Ceramics
Berlin, Germany
Curated ceramic goods from small-scale sustainable production.
___bonceramics.com

Broste Copenhagen
Copenhagen, Denmark
Democratic ceramic objects from jugs to egg cups in Nordic signature design. Also offers home textiles, candles, decorative items, and upholstered furniture.
___brostecopenhagen.com

Cristina Celestino
Milan, Italy
Italian design exploring colors, shapes, art, and design, embedded in both the traditional and the contemporary.
___cristinacelestino.com
pp. 52–55

Gien
Gien, France
Faïence manufacturing, using traditional undisclosed recipes, with over two centuries of experience.
___gien.com

Herriot Grace
Toronto, Canada
Hand-carved wooden objects, exclusive porcelain, and stoneware.
___herriottgrace.com

Jonathan Adler
New York, United States
Luxury ceramics that are designed seriously without taking themselves too seriously, from vases to bowls and ceramic objects Also offers upholstered furniture, cabinets, pillows, rugs, and lighting.
___jonathanadler.com

Keramische Werkstatt Margarethenhöhe
Essen, Germany
Handmade, minimalistic ceramic objects in soft pastel colors and classic forms with elaborate glazes.
___kwm-1924.de

KH Würtz
Horsens, Denmark
Hand-thrown and hand-glazed designs, often found in restaurants, galleries, and retails shops.
___khwurtz.dk

Klaus Dupont
Berlin, Germany
Eclectic figurines of animals, shells, and sea fans, drawing inspiration from the so-called Wunderkammer exhibits of the seventeenth century.
___klaus-dupont.com

Kristallglasmanufaktur Theresienthal
Theresienthal, Germany
Handmade crystalware, using extraordinary forms and bright colors which consolidate tradition and zeitgeist.
___theresienthal.de

La Double J.
Milan, Italy
Specialized in flamboyant contemporary tableware and linen. Also offers vintage clothing and accessories, homeware and jewelry.
___ladoublej.com

Laboratorio Paravicini
Milan, Italy
Custom-made ceramic dinnerware with detailed, illustrative decorations, indelible, non-toxic, and dishwasher safe.
___paravicini.it
pp. 168–171

Lobmeyr
Vienna, Austria
Glass creations and small glass elements since the nineteenth century, producing crafted details with subtle shine. Also offers lighting, especially chandeliers.
___lobmeyr.at

Lyngby Porcelæn
Lyngby, Denmark
Elegant and minimalistic glass and ceramic vases, pitchers, and bonbonnieres. Also offers decor and lighting.
___lyngbyporcelain.com

mpgmb
Montréal, Canada
Fun and affordable vases, étagères, and bowls. Also offers tables, clocks, and pet houses.
___mpgmb.com

Non Sans Raison
Limoges, France
Elegant, sometimes experimental porcelain and tableware for hotels, high-end restaurants, and concept stores with graphical design concepts.
___nonsansraison.com

Porzellanmanufaktur Nymphenburg
Munich, Germany
High-quality design techniques, from the Rococo to renowned modern designers. Also offers figures, jewelry, performances, and artist talks.
___nymphenburg.com
pp. 224–229

Siècle Paris
Brie, France
Porcelain and tableware made with techniques from the decorative arts in colors and motifs of past civilizations.
___siecle-paris.com

Skultuna
Skultuna, Sweden
Brass and metal works in minimalistic Swedish design, with four centuries of experience. Also offers chandeliers, bracelets, and cuffs.
___skultuna.com

Tadeáš Podracký
Prague, Czech Republic
Works at the intersection of arts and crafts, collaborating with different brands, producing artistic objects made of glass, metal, and natural materials, as well as lighting.
___tadeaspodracky.com
pp. 152–153

Tortus Copenhagen
Copenhagen, Denmark
Hand-thrown, minimalistic ceramic vessels and bowls of all sizes, made in small-scale production, using traditional and time-tested methods.
___tortus-copenhagen.com

Vista Alegre
Ílhavo, Portugal
Playful handmade porcelain and crystal works since 1824, using traditional techniques, and made in award-winning collaborations with both renowned designers and emerging artists. Also offers home décor.
___vistaalegre.com

Porzellanmanufaktur Nymphenburg

Schotten & Hansen in Bavaria, Germany, enjoys an international reputation for its high quality and sustainable woodwork, from floorboards and veneer paneling to staircases, doors, and furniture pieces.

Mindful Woodwork

After learning about furniture restoration by working in his father's auction house, Danish-born Torben Hansen set off to discover the world, which led him to Bavaria, Germany, where he co-founded Schotten & Hansen in 1984 at the age of 23. Developing expertise in materials research, craft tradition, and intelligent technology, the company has become one of the most renowned international specialists in wooden flooring and interiors. "I've developed an elaborate method that allows my products to sustain their natural benefits, to mature and age in a beautiful way, while meeting state-of-the-art building and design requirements. Through mindful observation and patience, I try to be an intermediary between nature and architecture," explains Hansen. With colors inspired by nature, he embraces the signs of aging and wear on a material, following the Japanese wabi-sabi view of aesthetics; it holds that true beauty lies in authenticity rather than in artificial perfection. ✕

Co-founder Torben Hansen (right page) with layers of oak used to manufacture technically superior floorboards that are durable, resistant to swelling and shrinkage, and free from solvents and formaldehyde.

Moon 01 is designed by Teo Yang for Savoir Beds, in copper linen with folding outer panels (right).

Sleeping Beauties

People spend about one third of their lives sleeping, so finding the right bed is very important. Some of the world's most luxurious beds are created by London-based Savoir Beds. The company was started in 1905 as The Savoy Bedworks with the aim of giving guests of the exclusive Savoy Hotel in London the best night's sleep. In 1997 it was relaunched as Savoir Beds under the ownership of Alistair Hughes and Stephen Winston, who have upheld the brand's standards of excellence. Handmade in the U.K., a Savoir bed consists of a box spring in a wooden frame, a mattress, and a topper. Savoir uses the finest natural materials in its beds, such as precious Argentinean horse tail hair, Mongolian cashmere, British lamb's wool, and soft cotton, combined for the perfect sleeping environment tailored to a client's needs. Curled horse tail hair provides unparalleled bounce and wicks away moisture, helping to regulate the sleeper's body temperature. Hand-tied springs in the mattress and base provide optimal support, while bespoke upholstery and headboards offer ultimate customization. ✗

FURNITURE UPHOLSTERY   Savoir Beds

Harlech 09 is designed by Madeline Weinrib and upholstered in Weinrib's Bara Black & Hazelnut and Black Foxtrot textile patterns (right page).

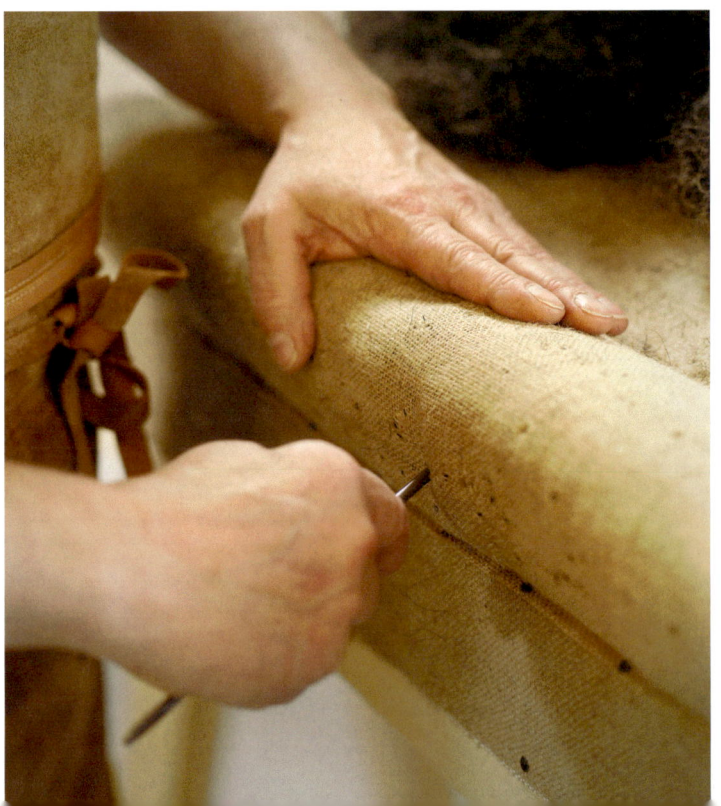

Savoir Beds   FURNITURE UPHOLSTERY   183

Winston 04 is designed by Mandeep Dillon for Savoir Beds and upholstered in aniline leather (left page).

Patrick Frey with his sons Pierre (named after his grandfather, who established the firm), Matthieu and Vincent, who are all company executives (bottom).

Braquenié

Fabrics in Family Hands

With Braquenié Parisian luxury fabrics and wallpaper house Pierre Frey successfully weaves the past with the future to create a unique blend of tradition and innovation.

A lot of the things we surround ourselves with are designed to stay with us for only a short time, from to-go coffee cups to fast fashion. There are few truly unique objects that we hold on to for decades, let alone save for the next generation. Perhaps this is why we cherish such products, those that come with a rich history—the heirlooms, the treasured finds from a vintage market. Family-owned companies that have survived throughout the decades, that have been around long enough to acquire some history, are becoming few and far between. One such company is Paris-based Pierre Frey. Founded in 1935, it is famous for its fabrics, wallpapers, and carpets. In 1991, Pierre's son Patrick Frey took the reins, adding another rich layer of history by buying the archives of Braquenié, the prestigious atelier that supplied the upper class of nineteenth-century France with opulently printed fabrics.

Why did you want to add Braquenié to the Pierre Frey brands?

For many years, I worked alongside my father. And all my life, I'd heard that Braquenié has the best collection of traditional French fabrics in the world. When I was around 40, I thought: what could I, his only kid, give him in return for passing down his company to me? So I tried to buy Braquenié. It took 10 years until I finally succeeded; by then my father was 90 years old, and would actually die six months later. But he still came to visit the famous archives himself, opening all the drawers and seeing what he had dreamt of his whole life.

In what way has the acquisition changed Pierre Frey?

The company got roots! Which I always considered to be very important, even for Pierre Frey, which was created in 1935. To have a history that reaches back as far as the late seventeenth century is absolutely fantastic for us.

YOU DON'T HAVE TO LIVE IN A HISTORIC BUILDING TO APPRECIATE CLASSIC DESIGN.

How did you experience stepping into Braquenié's archives for the first time?
I never thought there could be so many beautiful things in drawers—all of them revealed beauties. Someone from the archive was explaining everything: "This was done for the king, this was for the Rothschild family," and so on. Everything was there: the late nineteenth century, the French Empire, Louis XIV and XV. And it included a lot of cotton and linen fabrics, which was interesting because Braquenié was not a silk company.

Why was that?
It was the preferred material for Queen Marie Antoinette who, in her desire to escape as much from Versailles as possible, sometimes preferred simpler things. And she loved the predecessor of Braquenié, Oberkampf, founded by a German printer who imported all these incredible Indian prints and redesigned them for the Queen. Only later, around 1830, the family Braquenié bought the legendary archives. When the company was founded in the early 1820s, it specialized in handmade carpets. During the Second French Empire, prints became hugely popular and drove the success of Braquenié, which continued until the First World War.

Where do you produce the carpets today?
At our partner factory in the Alsace, the east of France, which has been doing this for generations. Recently, I received a parcel with the original of a print from 1855 that is still a part of our collection. Braquenié isn't a question of fashion; it's timeless.

But some things must have changed since then…
Oh yes, quite a few. Especially the colors. Thanks to modern chemistry they have greatly improved.

Curtains made in our age… you can keep them forever. Back then, the colors would have faded within a few years. Also, the quality of the backgrounds is much better. Today, we print on beautiful cottons and linens. In the old days, these were imported from India or China and were very irregular and full of straw. It had a certain charm, but people today

would not have accepted this. However, the printing technique hasn't really changed—everything is still done by hand.

How is that done?
Each design is separated into its colors. That leaves us with up to nine screens, and one after the other will be printed onto the fabric, always wet on dry. The result: perfect definition.

And how is that handled with the carpets?
They are totally handmade, upon request only. Most of them in Belgium, some in Asia. We have such a vast collection of carpet designs in the archive. Across the nineteenth century, there were 22 carpet designers in total, who left us thousands of exquisite documents.

Do you know if your clients live mostly in old, historic buildings, or in modern homes too?
Honestly, both. Sometimes I'm surprised by how young the people are who are buying Braquenié—some of our clients are in their early thirties. Today, you don't have to live in a historic building to appreciate a classic design. It's like in fashion—you can mix everything. I feel that younger generations are more open to combining things such as an eighteenth-century commode with a very modern painting. And that is just great.

An iconic toile de jouy—a traditional, usually pastoral-themed colored pattern that is repeated on a light background (bottom).

All three of your sons work with you. How have you taught them about the business?
Drop by drop. Quality is not embodied in only our fabrics, but also in the way we eat, the products we look at. Aren't we lucky to live in countries where culture is everywhere? The only thing you have to do with your kids is to take them to places where that quality is.

Did you learn this from your father?
And my mum. She was a designer and took me everywhere. All the time she would tell me, "Look at this store, look at this roof, look at this window." She would stop the car to look at a rainbow. In France we say, "A lot of people look, but very few people see."

You are both a businessman and a designer. How do you combine these two identities?
In the end, I am my own judge. If something doesn't sell, I can't fire a designer, because I did it. I think our job is to come up with very unusual, incredible things. My dad always told me the same thing, "Do what you believe in and never listen to anyone." After that: good luck.

Textiles & Wallpaper

Ailanto Design
Pratomagno, Italy
Hand-drawn wallpapers and fabrics, inspired by Tuscan landscapes. Also offers furniture designs.
___ailantodesign.com

Antoinette Poisson
Paris, France
Handmade domino wallpaper, printed and hand-colored fabric, design, and interior decoration. Also offers stationery.
___antoinettepoisson.com

Braquenié
Paris, France
Wallpaper and fabric design inspired by French décor and classicism. Also offers custom-made furniture and living accessories.
___pierrefrey.com
pp. 184–191

Ailanto Design

Calico
New York, United States
Contemporary marble-technique wallpaper design. Also offers fabric and soft home furnishings.
___calicowallpaper.com

Clarence House
London, United Kingdom
Handscreen printing of fabrics and wallpapers with high-style textures and hand-loomed brocades. Also offers trimmings as well as crewel embroidery.
___clarencehouse.com
pp. 104–107

Cole & Son
London, United Kingdom
Richly ornamented designer and printed wallpapers, in a wide selection of floral and stripe designs.
___cole-and-son.com

Declercq Passementiers
Paris, France
Specialized in handmade trimmings, luxurious tassels, braids, fringes, pompoms, and tie-backs. Also offers decoration accessories.
___declercqpassementiers.fr

Dedar
Appiano Gentile, Italy
Haute-couture fabrics, woven with luxurious yarns, featuring decorative as well as graphic patterns. Also offers wallpapers and cladding.
___dedar.com

Designers Guild
London, United Kingdom
Decorative and woven fabrics that use vibrant colors and intricate patterns. Also offers furniture and home accessories.
___designersguild.com

Houlès

Edelman Leather
New Milford, United States
Luxurious leather upholstery and leather rugs. Also offers floor and wall tiles, wallpapers, and home accessories.
___edelmanleather.com

Edmond Petit
Paris, France
Velvets and other textures, woven in the classic French tradition, featuring designs by Madeleine Castaing. Also offers drapery and trimmings.
___edmond-petit.fr

Élitis
Toulouse, France
Contemporary designs for wall tiles and wallpapers. Also offers home accessories and furniture.
___elitis.fr

Ellisha Alexina
Boston, United States
Handmade fabrics that blend polychromatic screen printing and hand painting.

Also offers custom-made designs.
___ellishaalexina.com

Emily Humphrey
Yorkshire, United Kingdom
Printed fabrics with generous, vintage-inspired ornaments.
Also offers soft furnishings and print-injected vintage furniture.
___emilyhumphrey.co.uk

Fornasetti
Milan, Italy
Decorative art designs inspired by Surrealism.
Also offers ceramics, home accessories, and fragrances.
___fornasetti.com

Friederike Tebbe
Berlin, Germany
Color consulting and individual color concept development for clients such as Werkbund Berlin.
Also offers ceramics, home accessories, and fragrances.
___farbarchiv.de

Fromental
London, United Kingdom
Richly decorated fabrics and wallpapers with a distinctly British touch.
___fromental.co.uk
pp. 90–93

Gastón y Daniela
Madrid, Spain
High-end decorative textiles, featuring geometric and floral patterns.
Also offers special productions, both in textiles and furniture.
___gastonydaniela.com

Heritage Trimmings
Derby, United Kingdom
Specialized in contemporary, traditional,

Voutsa

and historic trimmings with a royal touch.
Also offers bespoke services and advice on style choice.
___heritagetrimmings.co.uk

Herron
Chicago, United States
Hand-woven textiles and custom-made home furnishings.
___studioherron.com

Houlès
Paris, France
High-end trimmings, fabric, and hardware in both traditional French as well as contemporary styles.
Also offers upholstery, supplies, and accessories.
___houles.com
pp. 68–71

House of Hackney
London, United Kingdom
Offers fabrics and wallpapers inspired by traditional British design and featuring distinctive patterns, ranging from floral to Art Deco. Also offers home accessories and furniture.
___houseofhackney.com

Ellisha Alexina

Inkiostro Bianco
Sassuolo, Italy
Vinyl and fiberglass wallpapers.
Also offers engraved parquet flooring.
___ inkiostrobianco.com

Jende Posamenten Manufaktur
Forst/Lausitz, Germany
Trimmings and tassels, produced with traditional equipment.
Also offers jewelry and fashion accessories.
___ jende-manufaktur.de
pp. 132–135

Klaus Haapaniemi
London, United Kingdom
Fabrics and home accessories inspired by Finnish folklore.
Also offers a selection of shawls, silks, and scarves.
___ klaush.com

Kustaa Saksi
Amsterdam, Netherlands
Original tapestries and printed fabrics, using detailed textures and rich color palettes to produce psychedelic and imaginative patterns.
Also offers installations and motion graphics.
___ kustaasaksi.com

Kvadrat
Copenhagen, Denmark
Innovative textiles for upholstery and home accessories.
Also offers acoustics and roller blinds.
___ kvadrat.de

Leitner Leinen
Ulrichsberg, Austria
High-quality linen fabrics.
Also offers homewear.
___ leitnerleinen.com

Liberty London
London, Großbritannien
London's most charming department store, built in 1875 and specialized in popping floral textiles including classic prints by William Morris.
___ libertylondon.com

Marimekko
Helsinki, Finland
Colorful floral prints since 1951, suited for upholstery and decoration. Also offers fashion, bags, accessories and homeware.
___ marimekko.com

Miss Print
Ingatestone, United Kingdom
Modern wallpaper designs with graphic patterns and screen-printed upholstery fabric. Also offers lampshades and window films.
___ missprint.co.uk

Nya Nordiska
Dannenberg, Germany
Innovative fabrics and textile wall panels, inspired by Scandinavian design.

Ailanto Design

Also offers textile glass.

___nya.com

Roi du Lac
Rome, Italy
Whimsical hand-designed wallpapers, featuring colorful patterns. Also offers candles and plates.

___roidulac.co.uk

pp. 158–161

Rubelli
Venice, Italy
Venetian fine textiles and wall coverings. Also offers home accessories and furniture.

___rubelli.com

Sandberg Wallpaper
Ulricehamn, Sweden
Hand-sketched sustainable wallpaper, inspired by the Swedish landscape and the nature immediately surrounding their rural studio.

___sandbergwallpaper.com

Sister Parish
New York, United States
Timeless wallpaper designs in the signature style of Sister Parish, the interior designer to decorate the Kennedy White House.

___sisterparishdesign.com

Svenskt Tenn
Stockholm, Sweden
Patterned and floral wallpapers, printed using traditional distemper printing. Also offers furniture and a variety of home accessories.

___svenskttenn.se

The Painted House
United Kingdom
DIY paint rollers and foam rollers as a clever alternative to wallpaper.

___the-painted-house.co.uk

Voutsa

Timorous Beasties
Glasgow, United Kingdom
Wall coverings, lampshades, cushions, and fabrics in diverse unique pattern styles, ranging from Victorian to contemporary. Also offers a whole range of furniture, rugs, and ceramics.

___timorousbeasties.com

Voutsa
New York, United States
Eclectic printed wallpapers and textile in bold colors and patterns. Also offers aprons, silk scarves, and kimonos.

___voutsa.com

pp. 220–223

Wayne Pate
New York, United States
A selection of wimsical yet sophisticated textile designs. Also offers paintings, silkscreen prints, and books.

___waynepate.com

Welter Manufaktur für Wandunikate
Berlin, Germany
Wallpaper and wall panels in a variety of materials, such as beads, crystals, minerals, resin, etc.

___welter-wandunikate.de

Fromental

Shaping Color in Glass

While color is often seen as a product's outermost decorative layer, Germans Ermičs turns this hierarchy on its head with his mesmerizing glass objects. "Instead of finishing a product by painting it, I started from color," he notes. Born in Latvia, Ermičs graduated in 2011 from the Design Academy in Eindhoven and launched his studio in Amsterdam in 2014. His fascination with glass and mirrors led him to investigate their chromatic qualities and shape. For his Shaping Color series, he approaches color as a three-dimensional object, asking, "What would it look like if I stretch, turn, or fold the color as if it was a three-dimensional shape?" His Ombré Glass series is inspired by the ever-changing spectrum of light in the sky. In his glass and mirrored objects, vibrant hues dissolve to other shades and levels of transparency, evoking childhood memories. "I grew up close to natural phenomena—sunsets, dawns, and misty mornings," he says. "These are the feelings and sensations I'm trying to convey in my work." ✕

Lison de Caunes

In Awe of Straw

Parisian artisan Lison de Caunes has saved the art of straw marquetry from becoming a craft of the past.

The grande dame of straw marquetries, Lison de Caunes, in her Parisian atelier (right). There, she and her team produce bespoke furniture pieces, such as side tables (above), but also wall and floor paneling.

Glancing at the golden rye straw being cut down on the old fields of Burgundy, one is unlikely to know that carefully selected culms await the honor of being transformed into a rare and intricate object or an ornament on a piece of furniture. But that is exactly what happens with the lucky few that make it into the hands of Lison de Caunes. The grande dame of straw marquetry has dedicated her life to this artisanry and has made her clients fall in love with it. What started as a one-woman restoration workshop in the center of Paris has grown, over the decades, into an atelier with a team of 12. De Caunes leads the team and often still designs and crafts the bespoke furniture pieces and wall and floor panels herself. With her mission to save the art of straw marquetry, she has revived the traditional technique with modern, graphic patterns, and vibrant colors inspired by the avant-garde glamour of Art Deco.

Some of the tools Lison de Caunes has inherited from her grandfather, who also practiced this craft (left). Vertically cut straws are being applied onto a surface and secured with cold wood glue (left page).

When you started out, nobody was producing straw marquetry anymore. What drew you to it?
Throughout my childhood, I was surrounded by the straw marquetry furniture of my grandfather André Groult. He had started out as an antiques dealer and then moved on to designing his own pieces of furniture and working with different materials. That was during the Art Deco period; and he started producing straw marquetry again. In his later years, I loved watching him in his studio. I even tried working with him but I was really too young. I have a picture of him in my workshop, so he is always watching over me.

So who taught you the skills?
Sadly, my grandfather died when I was still in school. He only left me some straw and some tools. After the war, this form of marquetry was completely forgotten. When I was 17, I studied old works and, in a way, I was experimenting on them. I took restoration jobs from antiques dealers that specialized in the Art Deco period and worked with galuchat (sharkskin) before focusing on straw marquetry. My first job was restoring a commode that belonged to Jean-Michel Frank, and that's when I realized that I loved straw marquetry.

What were these early years like for you?
I found it all very exciting and so beautiful. Straw itself is such a humble material, but in the form of a marquetry it is transformed into very precious,

STRAW IS SUCH A HUMBLE MATERIAL BUT THE MARQUETRY TRANSFORMS IT INTO SOMETHING VERY PRECIOUS.

Wall and floor paneling with straw marquetry in a New York residence (left) and for designer Patrice Nourissat (below). A Jean-Louis Deniot sideboard covered with Lison de Caunes' marquetry (left page).

refined things. I worked on pieces that were from anytime between the seventeenth century and the Art Deco period. Over the years, I discovered new ways of making marquetry. Once I trusted my own skills, which took a few years, I started to do my own creations.

on a wall panel or piece of furniture by flattening it like a ribbon, and secure it with cold wood glue. The beauty of the material is that you don't need a varnish. At the end, I only wax it. But all of this is very time-consuming. One square meter takes me about four days of work.

Has the technique changed a lot over the years?
Overall, it hasn't developed that much. The process is still the same as it was during the Art Deco period and even the eighteenth century. The only difference is the patterns. Techniques, straw, and even the tools haven't really changed.

So, how do you transform the plain culms into something so beautiful?
It starts with finding a supplier of exceptional rye straw; mine is in Burgundy. Once the bunches arrive here at the workshop, we might tinge them depending on the design. After that, they are ready to be worked with: I cut open each straw, apply it

The straw bunches may be tinged, depending on the design, in the Parisian atelier, to create vivid effects as in a gentle green for the flowers in this storage bench (below) or in an electric blue as for this side table (right page).

How does the straw age?
Very well! The wax protects the straw against humidity and dryness. I recently saw some pieces from the 1920s, and they haven't changed. You might think that straw is very fragile, but in fact it's very strong and resistant if it is handled with attention before you start applying it.

So you need to be very careful.
Yes, we don't work with electrical tools; everything is done by hand. You must be focused as the work is so precise. I am usually in a state in which my hands do the work almost by themselves, but my mind is switched off. That's why it's usually very quiet in the workshop.

Is it difficult to predict how a pattern will reflect light?
Straw plays a lot with light, so it is very important to lay the straw down for the light and to find patterns. The effect it has is very difficult to foresee. Depending on the direction of the straw, the light will blur differently.

Do you have a lot of time to try out new patterns?
Whenever I have a free moment, I create my own designs. I want to find new ways to work with the straw, new patterns, new colors. It is very exciting to improve. For example, recently I tried layering the straws in gold leaf for a new effect or to create a different patina like silver.

Why do you like to use bold, bright colors in your own designs?
Since I only work on order, I mostly decide the colors with the client beforehand. I have a lot of samples in my workshop which helps them make a decision. During the Art Deco period, a lot of things had been done such as coloring the straw and creating extraordinary shapes on the furniture. But there are so many more possibilities. That's why I try to use new colors and new patterns to show designers and decorators that straw can be very contemporary and modern.

Soft Skills

"Upholstery is an interesting area; it's something that we just sit on and take for granted, yet the pieces are the absolute anchor of a room, and the experience of sitting is something we think about here a lot," says Suzanne O'Flynn, managing and creative director of British furniture company John Sankey. Located in Derbyshire, the company designs and produces exceptional, handcrafted upholstered furniture based on historical shapes but designed for contemporary living. Founded in the 1950s, the company has been family-run since 1992, with each new generation of the same family making its furniture through the years. John Sankey offers a lifetime guarantee on all of its wooden frames and springs, which are produced strictly in-house. It also works with mills around the world to source and develop a wide variety of fine fabrics, which combine with their many forms for myriad possibilities of expression. According to O'Flynn, "Comfort is so subjective, so we really try to think through what people might need."

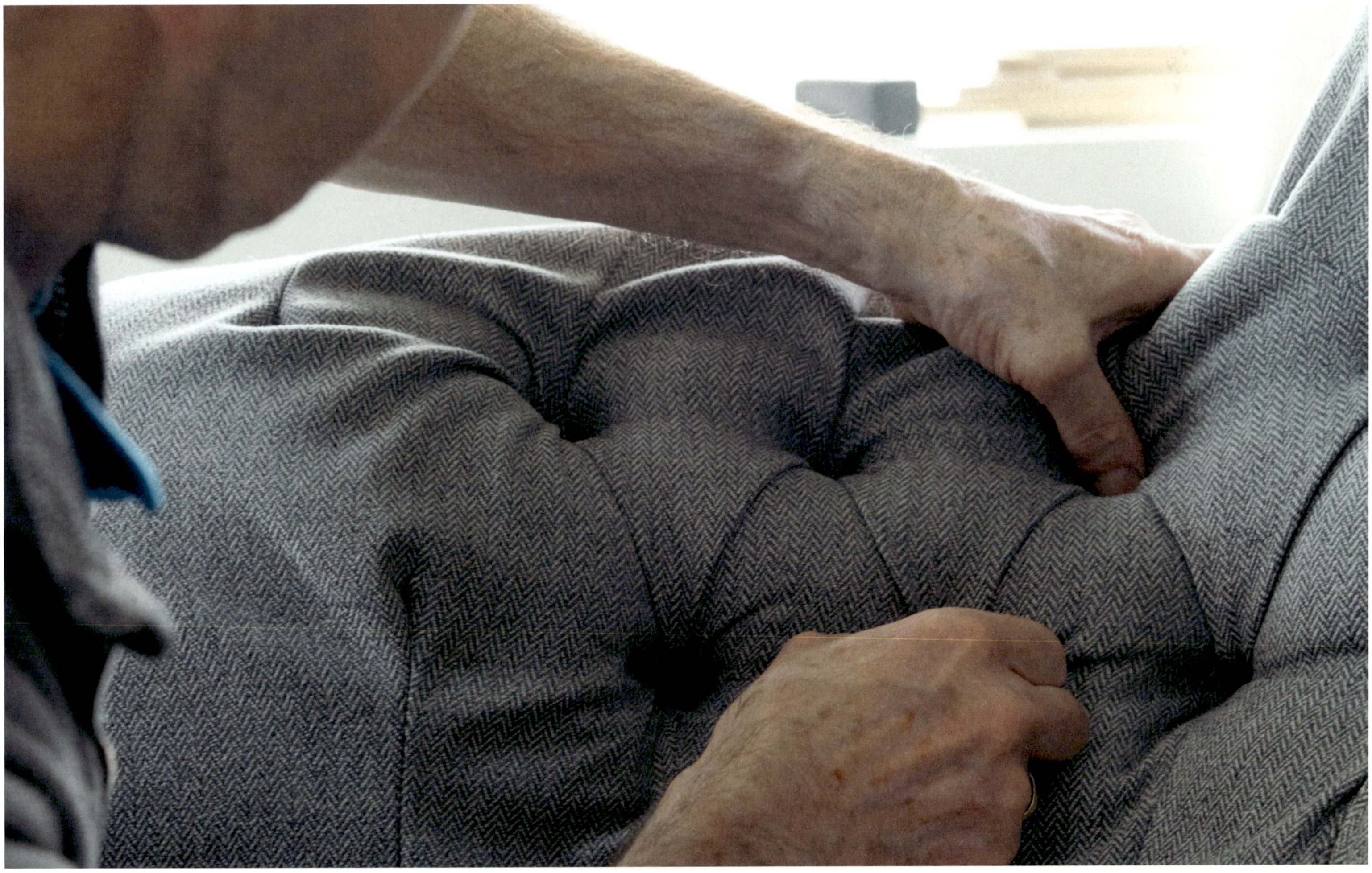

John Sankey's luxury sofas, chairs, and ottomans are hand-crafted to order in Long Eaton in the East Midlands of England, and come with a lifetime guarantee on their frames and springs.

Tiled In

Designed in Toulouse and produced by master tile makers in Morocco, Ateliers Zelij tiles draw inspiration from traditional north African patterns, Art Deco, as well as contemporary graphic design.

The Arabic word for tile, *zellige*, or *zellij*, refers to the colorful, intricate mosaics of geometric tiles closely associated with Morocco and Moorish culture, which spread from northern Africa to Spain and Italy during the Middle Ages. Now Ateliers Zelij is reinterpreting this centuries-old craft for the twenty-first century. Delphine Laporte and Samir Mazer joined forces in 2000 while studying industrial design in Toulouse. Laporte, with a background in interior design, and Mazer, with a background in sculpture, channel their shared passion for surfaces and Moroccan culture, fusing traditional craftsmanship with a contemporary design vision. With studios in France and Morocco, they are close to their clients as well as the master tile makers they work with in Morocco. Their repertoire includes both terracotta and cement tiles in a broad range of heritage and contemporary patterns, colors, and textures. Refining age-old methods ensures consistency while maintaining unique subtleties in color and tone that arise from the artisanal process. ✕

Ateliers Zelij's new handmade sculptural tiles offer additional depth while playing with different shapes and colors (left).

Kitchens & Bathrooms & Tiles

Abimis
San Polo di Piave, Italy
Bespoke kitchens with a holistic approach. Also offers interior services for yachts and cruises.
___abimis.com

Agape Design
Mantua, Italy
Modern and minimalistic bathroom fixtures.

Atelier Dialect

Also offers homewares and storage solutions.
___agapedesign.it

Alape
Copenhagen, Denmark
A wide range of wash basins and self-standing sinks. Also offers lights, mirrors, and other bathroom fixtures.
___alape.de

Antonio Lupi
Florence, Italy
Extravagant bathroom fixtures with an architectural focus.
Also offers mirrors, lights, and other accessories.
___antoniolupi.it

Ateliers Zelij
Toulouse, France
Traditional or modern terracotta, ceramic, and cement tiles made in Morocco.
___zelij.com
pp. 212–215

Beauregard Design
Kiawah Island, United States
Full-service interior design with bright colors and bold textures.
___beauregarddesign.net

Bisazza
Montecchio Maggiore, Italy
Statement seats and tables with a strong textural palette, leading manufacturer of artificial mosaics in various styles. Also offers small-scale interior accessories.
___bisazza.it

Boffi
Lentate sul Seveso, Italy
Visionary, clean kitchens with classic Italian craftsmanship. Also offers fixtures for bathrooms and outdoor use.
___boffi.com

Bulthaup
Bodenkirchen, Germany
Pared-down tables with an emphasis on quality. Also offers striking chairs and benches.
___bulthaup.com

Ceramica Cielo
Fabrica di Roma, Italy
A variety of ceramic homewares for every room. Also offers bespoke shower trays.
___ceramicacielo.com

Emery & Cie

Ceramica Globo
Castel Sant'Elia, Italy
Modern rounded fixtures for contemporary bathrooms.
___**ceramicaglobo.com**

Cocoon
Amsterdam, Netherlands
Bathroom collections with a timeless appeal.
Also offers standalone tubs.
___**bycocoon.com**

DeVol
Leicestershire, United Kingdom
Country living and Shaker style kitchens.
Also offers interior homeware.
___**devolkitchens.co.uk**

Devon&Devon
Florence, Italy
Striking bathroom appliances with statement faucets in various finishes.
Also offers graphic wallpapers.
___**devon-devon.com**

Dornbracht
Iserlohn, Germany
Spa-ready bathroom fixtures and Smart Water solutions..
Also offers utilitarian kitchen sinks.
___**dornbracht.com**

Ex.t
Florence, Italy
Playful, minimalistic outfittings for bathrooms—from tubs to mirrors.
Also offers modern storage.
___**ex-t.com**

Fantini
Pella, Italy
Sleek, graphic washroom and kitchen appliances.
Also offers basins and tubs.
___**fantini.it**

File under Pop
Copenhagen, Denmark
A wide range of tiles, textures, and wallpapers.
Also offers patterned homewares for every room.
___**fileunderpop.com**

Florim
Fiorano Modenese, Italy
Traditional Italian marble slabs.
Also offers luxurious furniture.
___**florim.com**

Golem Baukeramik
Berlin, Germany
Renovation and production of classic brick, marble, and ceramic wares.
Also offers wall tiles and terracotta accents.
___**golem-baukeramik.de**
pp. 264–269

Heath Ceramics
Sausalito, United States
Colorful wall ceramic wares for the kitchen.
Also offers sturdy bags and subtle jewelry.
___**heathceramics.com**

Humphrey Munson
Essex, United Kingdom
High-quality bespoke kitchens with made-to measure wooden cabinetry.
Also offers Limestone tiles.
___**humphreymunson.co.uk**

Ivanka
Kalaszi, Hungary
Concrete constructions and furniture.
Also offers architectural design and development.
___**ivankaconcrete.com**

Made a Mano
Copenhagen, Denmark
Design and production of Danish-Italian style high-end, handmade traditional and contemporary tiles..
___**madeamano.com**

Marrakech Design
Gothenburg, Sweden
Patterned cement tiling with geometric accents in French-Moroccan style.
Also offers tiles in a soft palette of colors.
___**marrakechdesign.se**

Emery & Cie

Golem

Minacciolo
Treviso, Italy
Chic kitchen outfittings in different styles—from country to modern minimalism. Also offers textured finishes for an English twist.
___minacciolo.com

Mipa Design
Casoni di Ravarino, Italy
Striking graphic tiles in a variety of styles.
___mipadesign.it

Modulnova
Prata di Pordenone, Italy
Specialised in full-service bespoke kitchens and bathrooms.
___modulnova.it

Mutina
Fiorano, Italy
Specialised in wall tiling in a broad palette of textures. Also offers outfittings for unique spaces.
___mutina.it

New Ravenna
Exmore, United States
Wall and floor coverings with a Renaissance twist or in playful modern styles. Also offers cut-to-order glass, stone, and ceramic mosaics.
___newravenna.com

Not Only White
Amsterdam, Netherlands
Flexible sanitary solutions. Also offers bathroom storage.
___notonlywhite.com

Piet Boon
Oostzaan, Netherlands
Multi-disciplinary design services for bath, kitchen, living areas, and bedrooms balancing functionality, aesthetics, and individuality.
___pietboon.com

Plain English
Suffolk, United Kingdom
High-quality cupboards and kitchens in a Georgian and Edwardian style.
___plainenglishdesign.co.uk

Popham Design
Marrakech, Morocco
Graphically patterned cement tiles produced by Moroccan artisans.
___pophamdesign.com

Popstahl
Berlin, Germany
Functional, modular, and sustainably custom-made kitchens.
___popstahl.de

SieMatic
Löhne, Germany
Purist, urban, and classic style kitchens.
___siematic.com

Valcucine
Pordenone, Italy
Innovative and functional kitchen collections and systems.
___valcucine.com

VIA
Bacharach, Germany
Cement mosaic tiles and terrazzo panels in traditional and modern styles.
___viaplatten.de

Victoria & Albert
Telford, United Kingdom
Traditional and modern baths and basins

Ateliers Zelij

made from QUARRYCAST®—a blend of Volcanic Limestone™ and high-performance resins—as well as taps and accessories.
___vandabaths.com

Vola
Horsens, Denmark
Bathroom fixtures and fittings, using, among others, original designs by Arne Jacobsen.
___vola.com

Decorations Paints

Anna von Mangoldt
Nieheim, Germany
Modern but timeless wall and furniture paint popular with designers and architects, with a range of 168 bold colors, containing an ecologically-friendly, high-pigmented chalk emulsion. Also offers workshops for repainting furniture.
___annavonmangoldt.com

Benjamin Moore
Montvale, United States
Specialized in manufacturing paint from their own resins and from proprietary waterborne colorants, helping to maintain viscosity in every color, durable finishes, and scrubbabilty.
___benjaminmoore.com

Caparol
Ober-Ramstadt, Germany
Decorative paints, including coatings and glaze, which are all emission- and solvent-free. Also offers composite heat insulation systems as well as built heritage conservation.
___caparol.de

Farrow & Ball
Dorset, United Kingdom
Luxury paints and wallpapers, 132 colors containing high-pigmented chalk and China clay emulsion, available in 11 finishes, all ecologically-friendly and inspired by traditional British wall colors and wallpapers.
___farrow-ball.com

Fine Paints of Europe
Woodstock, United States
Specialised in manufacturing thousands of colors, including exclusive Dutch paints, as well as Pantone paints and a color range developed by Martha Stewart.
___finepaintsofeurope.com

Flamant
Geraardsbergen, Belgium
Palette of 128 colors, from subtle to bold. Also offers a whole range of furniture, from tableware to seating.
___flamant.com

Jotun
Sandefjord, Norway
Decorative paints and performance coatings (marine, protective, and powder coatings) from all over the world.
___jotun.com

KT Color
Uster, Suisse
Production of 81 official Le Corbusier colors, manufacturing high-end paints for architects and architecture in over 120 pigments, including a variety of natural, mineral, and distemper paints. Also offers specialist seminars for clients and painters.
___ktcolor.ch

Little Greene
Manchester, United Kingdom
Very high-pigmented, ecologically-friendly paint, from mostly natural components, such as chalk and eggshell, inspired by traditional British wall colors and wallpapers.
___littlegreene.de

Friederike Tebbe

Clarence House

The Walls Are Alive

Imagine waking to a wall full of lips cavorting alongside the Ballet Russes, or relaxing among a school of larger-than-life koi. Under the motto "The Walls are Alive," Voutsa in New York City can help you do this and more with its eclectically printed wallpaper and textiles. The decorative design studio is the brainchild of George Venson. After studying economics and visual arts at Rice University in Texas, he moved to New York in 2008. The idea to produce wallpaper was born out of circumstance, when he decided to enliven his tiny studio with something beautiful. "I covered every wall of my apartment—including the ceiling—in painted lips, peacocks, and birds of paradise," he recounts. He launched Voutsa in 2013, offering hand-painted wallpaper commissions and wallpaper printed with patterns based on his own watercolor designs. Voutsa has since expanded to offer its audacious patterns on aprons, silk scarves, kimonos, and handmade luggage, produced in collaboration with workshops in Italy.

Voutsa offers fresh prints inspired by flora and fauna—such as the roll with palm leaves (below) or the plumes of ostrich feathers (right)—but also more abstract designs, as in the bedroom below left.

Ceramics from the Castle

The renowned Porzellan Manufaktur Nymphenburg in Bavaria, Germany, prides itself on producing fine porcelain entirely by hand. The conscious decision to not automate any processes ensures the unequalled delicacy and quality of its products. Master artisans use techniques that have been passed down and refined over the centuries since the company's founding in 1747. Even the porcelain paste is made on site according to a secret recipe of kaolin, feldspar, and quartz that is rolled until smooth and left to rest for two years, until it is ready for processing. Paints are prepared in the factory's own lab; and its porcelain painters work without templates. Turning and casting is always done by hand, and each ornament is individually applied. Nymphenburg's extensive repertoire ranges from historical designs dating back to the eighteenth century to contemporary, avant-garde, and custom figurines, tableware, and jewelry, developed in collaboration with distinguished artists, architects, and designers like Tobias Rehberger or Damien Hirst. ✕

Nymphenburg's master artisans use strictly manual production methods that have been passed down and refined since the company's founding in the eighteenth century.

228 TABLEWARE

Ania Bauer and Jacob Brinck are the co-founders of llot llov in Berlin (left). The Osis low table is designed for Gallery Bensimon (below).

Salted to Taste

The unique finishes on these interlocking side tables by Berlin-based design collective llot llov are the result of a chemical process between salt and spruce wood. Osis, the collection's name, points to the process of osmosis that occurs when salt is spread on a wet glazed timber surface. As the salt absorbs the surrounding liquids, it draws the pigment into the wood grain to create different patterns and gradients. The results are influenced by the kind of salt used, the size of the salt crystals, humidity, and the length of reaction time. Full wooden boards and bespoke furniture prepared according to the Osis technique are also available in three patterns and nearly any customized color. llot llov was founded in 2006 by Ania Bauer, Jacob Brinck, Lena Hirche, and Ramon Toshiro Merker, with Bauer and Brinck serving as heads of design since 2014. Their projects include interiors, design and production of serial products and individual pieces, and conceptual events that delve into art and culture. ✕

Salt applied to a glazed timber surface draws the pigment into the grain. Large crystals tend to create large patterns with strong contrasts, whereas fine salt crumbs trigger more differentiated patterns with softer gradients.

Bloc Studios

Marbleous

With the philosophy that each piece of stone contains a unique story waiting to be told, Bloc Studios in Italy transforms raw, salvaged marble into thoughtful everyday objects.

Marble has always been a part of your life, Sara. Do you remember your first visit to a quarry?
Oh, it was just amazing. I must have been around 12 years old. But to be honest, back then I couldn't really enjoy it—I was too scared of heights. Luckily enough, that fear got weaker over the years. When I visit a Carrara quarry today, I can feel the marble's purity. And with Bloc Studios we want to capture this feeling.

How did you meet Massimo?
My mother and his father own a business together that sells marble blocks. Both of us were working for them, realizing how much of the marble would actually never go on sale. Every month the cutting of the stone leaves us with a staggering 15,000 tons of waste—not all of it in an unusable condition. That's why we started to collect some of these leftovers, even before we founded Bloc Studios. Now that we are a few years in, Massimo and I have separated the tasks. He's doing all the physically demanding work like choosing the marble, transporting it to the workshop, and monitoring production. I, on the other hand, initiate the collaborations and lead the creative direction. But of course we constantly exchange ideas.

So how did the first collaborations come about?
We met our first partners, the Swiss duo Thévoz—Choquet, through a mutual friend. They had just graduated and were as new to the design world as

F

Few materials in recent years have enjoyed as high-impact a comeback as marble. For thousands of years, the stone has decorated homes—and palaces—and fascination for the material has never waned. With its latest revival, however, it has broken free from the luxury-realm cliches, thanks in part to designers who are carving it into progressive, minimal shapes and putting the material's fine grain and unique texture into focus. At the forefront of today's marble designs are Sara Ferron Cima and Massimo Ciuffi of Bloc Studios. With deep roots in the Italian marble capital, Carrara, their studio collaborates with international designers to craft truly modern objects and furniture pieces.

INSTEAD OF BEING HEAVY, LUXURIOUS, AND INTIMIDATING WE BELIEVE MARBLE NEEDS SIMPLICITY AND MINIMALISM.

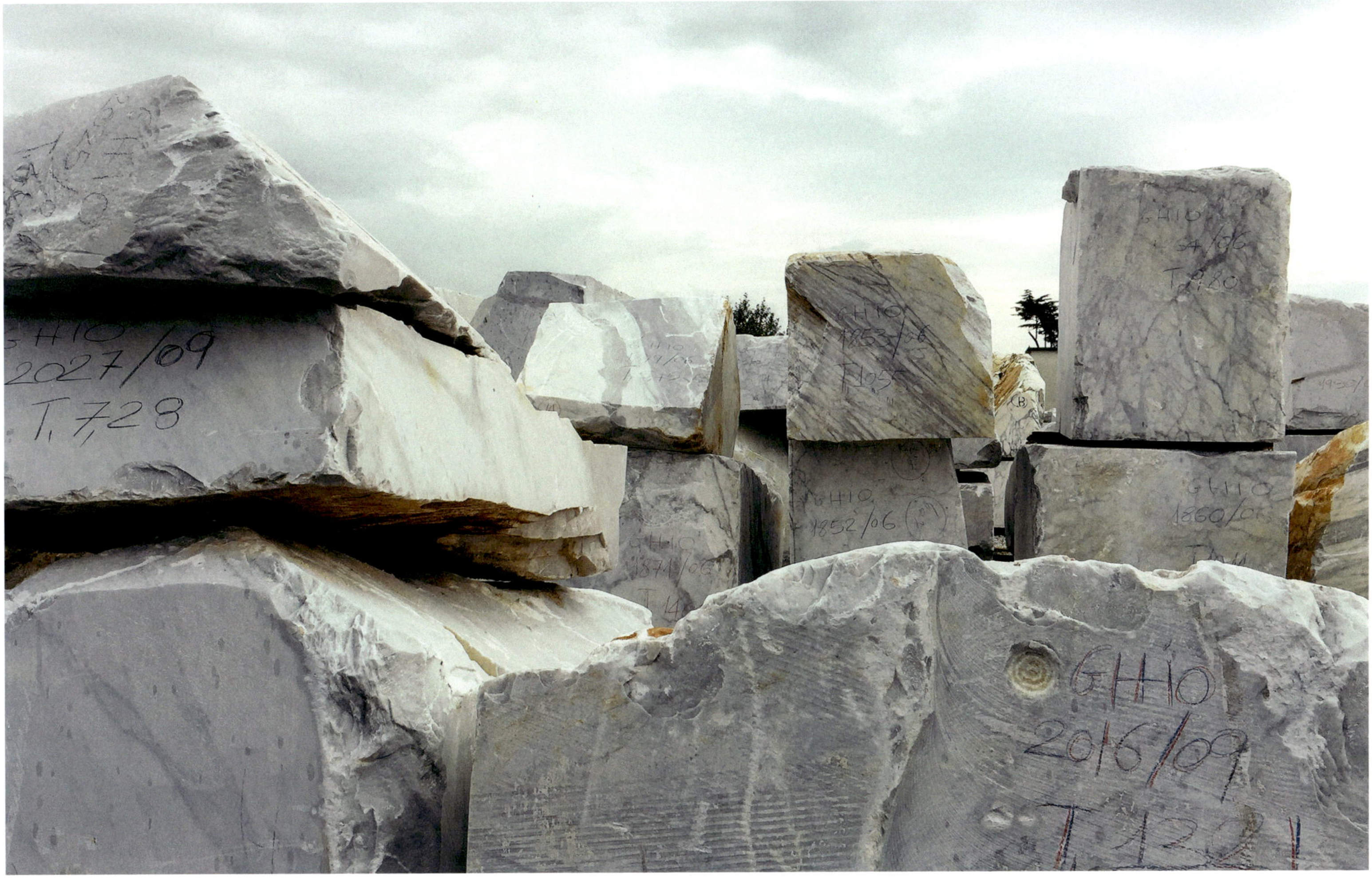
2027/09
T, 728
GHIO
2016/09

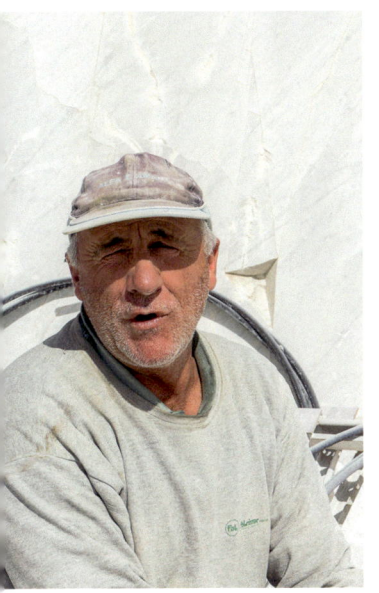

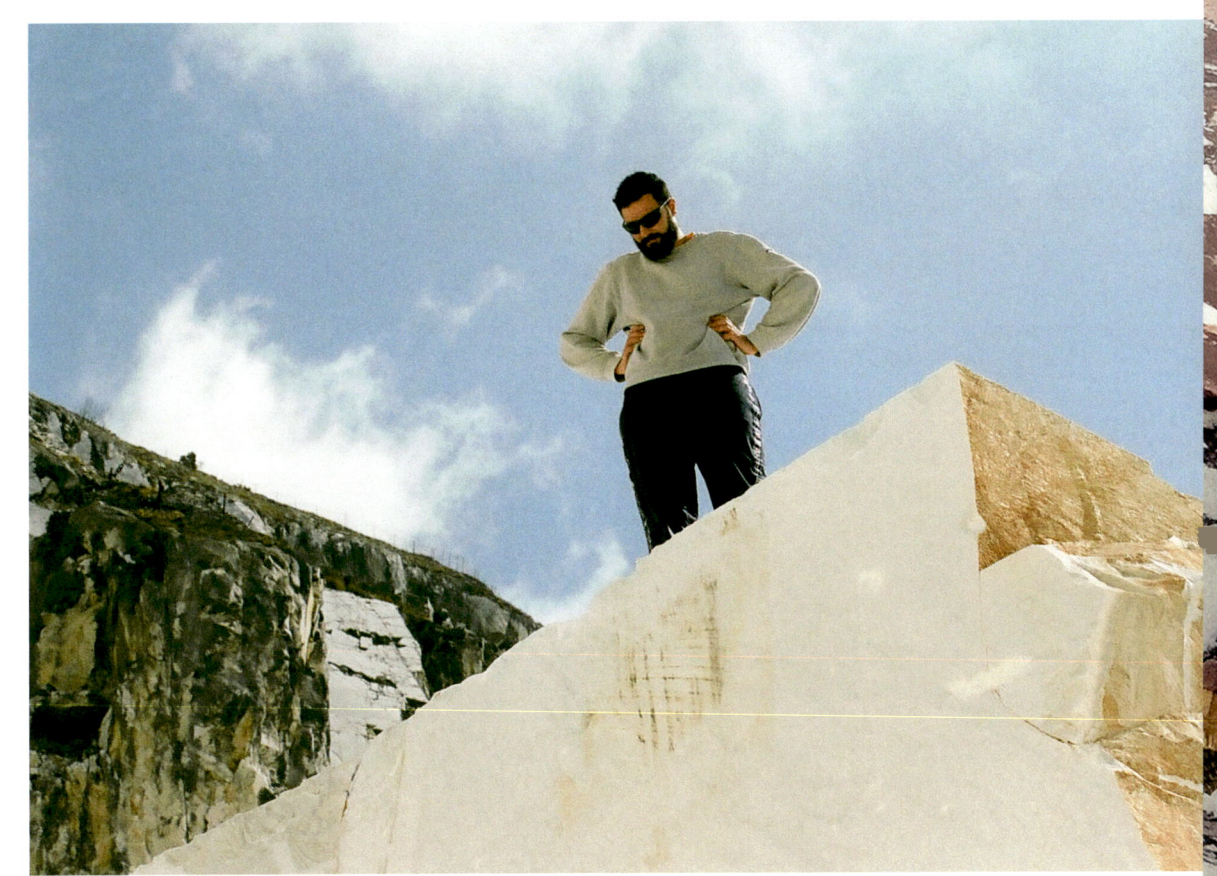

All Marmo Domestico products are available on request in other marble types and colors, and bespoke sizes and variations. Each piece of marble is unique due to its natural diversity.

we were, so everything felt very fresh, almost like a start-up. Together we developed a range of furniture pieces and objects, which, to our surprise, not only received great feedback from the press but also got picked up by a few very nice galleries. That encouraged us to continue.

Do you usually approach the designers?
It depends. After a collaboration with the magazine Apartamento, a lot of designers actually wanted to work with us. But I still reach out to people I find interesting. That was the case with Carl Kleiner. I adored his photo series *Posture* featuring single flowers shot in very artistic positions, so I asked him if he would want to bring his beautiful images into the real world. The result was these lovely vases. As a matter of fact, we never simply hand over a brief to somebody; we want it to be a fusion of ideas, ours and the designers'.

Do you need to educate the designers about the can- and can't-dos of marble?
Yes, most of them haven't worked with it before and don't know its limits. They have all these exciting ideas, but we can't realize them. While the CNC machines and robots cutting the stone can do almost anything, the final product wouldn't be close to affordable.

Is all the manufacturing done by machines?
The cutting yes, but the finishes are done manually with the help of local artisans. There's no design that hasn't been touched by a pair of hands, even the simplest ones. And all of this happens in Italy.

The Posture series (this page and right page bottom) has been developed in collaboration with the photographer Carl Kleiner. The Voie Lights (right page top) consist of neon lights and marble blocks and investigate the manipulation of light-paths.

IMPERFECTIONS LAY IN THE NATURE—MARBLE IS AN ORGANIC MATERIAL.

What's so special about the marble from Carrara?
It's the whitest marble and it has so many varieties: Classic Bianco, Statuario, Arabescato, and so on, all beautiful and fairly easy to work with. A lot of the colored stones are too hard to process so you can only use them as floor pavements. White marble holds this balance between soft and hard with a perfect grain. And in terms of style, it's an evergreen. But we import marble from all over the world: Northern Africa, China, France, Spain, and Turkey.

Why do you think marble is so popular again?
Everybody on this planet buys so many products that are exactly the same. But marble gives you this sense that you bought something unique. Even if it's just a small object like a vase, you won't see its grain anywhere else. The beauty is that every piece is different. Marble is unpredictable.

How do you pick the stones?
As we are trying to use as much leftover marble as possible, the only criterion is that the stone isn't cracked. Other imperfections lay in the nature—it's an organic material. A small hole or a little defect shouldn't deem it unusable. That's why we focus on the shape. Here in Italy, all the marble is connected to the past—that can be a church or buildings in an old town—and it comes across as heavy, luxurious, and intimidating. Very inaccessible. That's why we believe marble needs simplicity and minimalism.

Do you consider it to be a luxurious material?
As my family has been trading with marble now for three generations, marble is to me as normal as a loaf of bread. But of course, it's luxurious; so much effort goes into a product made from marble, from the workers cutting the stone out of the mountain and into blocks, to the big trucks rushing down small streets through the mountains, to the recutting at our depot.

Joogii Design

Furniture Metal & Glass

Antique Mirror
Siena, Italy
Colored and patterned mirrors and glass sheets and tiles.
___antiquemirror.it

AYTM
Aarhus, Denmark
Danish-designed luxury home accessories made of blown glass, brass, and copper. Also offers carpets, side tables, wooden and textile accessories.
___aytm.dk

Dennis Slootweg
The Hague, Netherlands
Rusted metal furniture, especially cabinets and cupboards, made from recycled materials such as industrial waste.
___dennisslootweg.nl

Dimitri Bähler
Biel, Switzerland
Interior accessories related to installations (vases, bowls, and hooks), and collaborations with a variety of well-known furniture labels such as HAY.
___dimitribaehler.ch

Eric Trine
Long Beach, United States
Locally designed and produced furniture and home objects in a classic California modern style.
___erictrine.com

Germans Ermičs
Amsterdam, Netherlands
Colorful, experimental ombré glass mirror furniture.
___germansermics.com
pp. 196–199

Glas Italia
Macherio, Italy
Production of luxurious, minimalistic glass home furnishings handmade by Italian master glassmakers.
___glasitalia.com

Guillermo Santomà
Cornellà, Spain
Product and interior design, working with bold colors and various materials, such as sand, glass, metal, and neon.
___guillermosantoma.com

Het Tafelbureau
Wassenaar, Netherlands
Tables handcrafted in their own blacksmith atelier.
___hettafelbureau.nl

James Stickley
London, United Kingdom
Simple and functional bold furniture pieces in graphic minimal style—from sideboards to lighting
___jamesstickley.co.uk

Joogii Design
Los Angeles, United States
Bridging the gap between object, art, fashion, and music, such as, for example, an iridescent collection of geometrical glass furniture inspired by Daft Punk.
___joogiidesign.com

Marcin Rusak
London, United Kingdom
Multidisciplinary design, working with the idea of ephemerality, reusing flower waste as a decorative element.
___marcinrusak.com
pp. 46–51

Muller van Severen
Ghent, Belgium
Specialized in minimalist sling chairs

Cristina Celestino

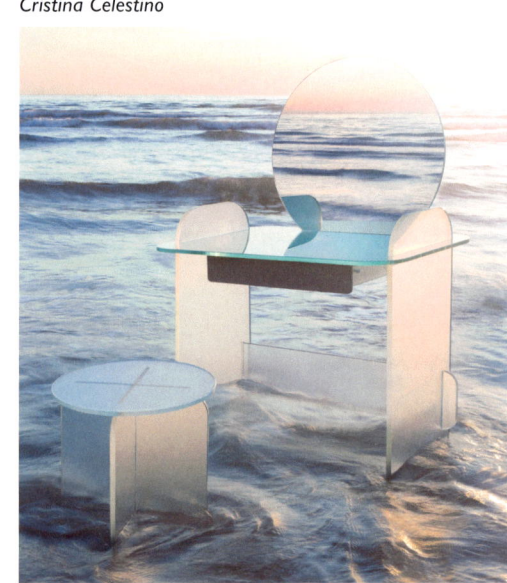

and shelves in bold colors.
___mullervanseveren.be
pp. 118–121

Overgaard & Dyrman
Copenhagen, Denmark
Contemporary Danish design, merging traditional craft techniques and modern technology to create a collection of wire steel chairs, sofas, stools, and tables.
___oandd.dk

Pedro Paulo-Venzon
Florianópolis, Brazil
Tropical modernist metal furniture, inspired by the architecture of Brazil's colonial past.
___pedrovenzon.com

Schellmann Art+Furniture
Munich, Germany
Micro-architectural, industrial inspired furniture in metal frames. Also offers wooden tables, benches, and seating units.
___schellmannart.com

Schmiede Münks
Meerbusch, Germany
Blacksmith working with minimalist, industrial, and modernist designs.
___schmiede-muenks.de

Studio Truly Truly
Rotterdam, Netherlands
Furniture at the interface of art and industry by graphic-turned-object-designers. Also offers lighting, textiles, rugs, wallpaper, and sofas for IKEA.
___studiotrulytruly.com

Swedish Ninja
Vejle, Denmark
Sustainable and functional home products by Swedish designer Maria Gustavsson. Also offers mixed material furniture (metal, cork, wood, paper, and leather).
___swedishninja.com

Tolix
Voorschoten, Netherlands
Light and functional vintage-style industrial design steel furniture.
___tolix.de

Victoria Wilmotte
Paris, France
Sculptural products, ranging from home accessories, lamps to furniture.
___victoriawilmotte.fr
pp. 36–41

Furniture Stone

Bloc Studios
Carrara, Italy
Simple and functional home accessories made from salvaged raw marble blocks.
___bloc-studios.com
pp. 234–241

Brooksbank & Collins
London, United Kingdom
Multidisciplinary design, from jewelry to textiles and tableware.
___brooksbankcollins.com

Budri
Mirandola, Italy
Marble manufacturer, collections in collaboration with renowned designers and brands.
___budri.com

DWA Design Studio
Milan, Italy
Interior and product design in collaboration with fashion and design brands.
___dw-a.i
pp. 128–131

Bloc Studios

Lapicida
Harrogate, United Kingdom
Bespoke tiles and stone pieces, 3D objects, and waterjet cut design.
___lapicida.com

Marsotto Edizioni
Bovolone, Italy
Minimalistic Carrara marble furniture and home accessories, exclusively black and white, by, for example, British architect David Chipperfield
___edizioni.marsotto.com

Olivia Aspinall Studio
Nottingham, United Kingdom
Handmade Jesmonite vessels and tables in different patterns.
___olivia-aspinall.com

On Entropy
London, United Kingdom
Delicate marble creations, from furniture to small accessories.
___onentropy.co.uk

Paulsberg Habitat
Dresden, Germany
Elegant concrete furniture and accessories Also offers concrete toys and jewelry.
___store.paulsberg.co

Built-Ins

Arquitectura-G
Barcelona, Spain
Interior design with clean and strong geometries for functional rooms and objects.
___arquiteturag.wordpress.com

Atelier Dialect
Deurne, Netherlands
Durable universal designs for kitchen units, shelving systems, and more.
___atelierdialect.be
pp. 250–251

Bartmann Berlin
Berlin, Germany
Traditionally and locally crafted contemporary functional designs, focusing on kitchen and closet solutions as well as furniture.
___bartmannberlin.de

Beadboard
Plochingen, Germany
American/Scandinavian country style wooden wall cladding.
___beadboard.de

Framework Studio

Crosby Studios
Moscow, Russia
Offer avant-garde interior and product design in fresh colors and playful minimalistic forms.
___crosby-studios.com
pp. 64–67

Emmanuelle Simon
Paris, France
Specialized in interior and product design with light colors and natural materials, such as linen and rope.
___emmanuellesimon.com

Framework Studio
Amsterdam, Netherlands
Interior design with unique materials and artisanal techniques with a stylistic variety, ranging from Neo-Baroque to Art Deco to Graphic Modernism.
___framework.eu

Garde Hvalsøe
Copenhagen, Denmark
Cabinetry in the Scandinavian tradition, wooden kitchens, bathroom furniture, and more.
___gardehvalsoe.dk
pp. 154–157

Københavns Møbelsnedkeri
Copenhagen, Denmark
Design and production of beautifully detailed and highly functional furniture in the classical Scandinavian style. Also offers metalwork and leather upholstery.
___kbhsnedkeri.dk
pp. 30–35

Lala Architectes
Bordeaux, France
Convert and decorate old und new buildings and interiors.
___lala-architectes.com

Martin Holzapfel
Berlin, Germany
Furniture in reduced forms, straight lines, and bold colors.
___martinholzapfel.com

SCEG Architects
Turin, Italy
Interior design in bold colors, reinterpreting traditional Italian elegance.
___sceg.it

Thomas Schmitter
Munich, Germany
Wooden furniture and built-ins for a Bishop's residence, a Baroque castle, an Art Nouveau villa, and the like.
___thomasschmitter.de

Wolfgang Koentopp
Bissendorf, Germany
Façades, fittings, and furniture. Also offers design and planning for stone, stucco, metal, glass, mosaic, and paint works.
___wolfgang-koentopp.de

Radiators & Fireplaces

Antrax
Resana, Italy
Designer radiators and heated towel racks, made in collaborations with Matteo Thun, Daniel Libeskind, and others.
___antrax.it

Bisque
Surrey, United Kingdom
Radiators in a variety of styles, finishes, and colors.
___bisque.co.uk

Cinier
Sete, France

Modern design radiators and towel warmers.
Also offers fan coils and LED lighting.
___cinier.com

Foursteel
Aveiro, Portugal
Minimalist (stainless) steel design radiators and towel warmers.
___foursteel.eu

Jøtul
Fredrikstad, Norway
Cast-iron stoves and fireplaces, handmade by Norwegian craftsmen.
___jotul.com

La Castellamonte
Castellamonte, Italy
Traditionally crafted ceramic fireplaces and woodstoves.
___lacastellamonte.it

Paladin Radiators
New York, United Kingdom
Traditional cast-iron radiators.
___paladinradiators.com

Period House Store
Richmond, United Kingdom
Cast-iron radiators and fireplaces.
Also offers period furniture and lighting, flooring, doors, and traditional electrical fittings.
___periodhousestore.co.uk

Reina
Great Yeldham, United Kingdom
Innovative designer radiators and heated towel rails.
___reinadesign.co.uk

Scirocco
Gattico, Italy
Italian design radiators and towel warmers.
___sciroccoh.it

Emery & Cie

Skantherm
Oelde, Germany
Modern design-oriented fireplaces and steel furnaces.
___skantherm.de

Terma
Gdansk, Poland
Radiators and heating elements and accessories.
___termaheat.com

The Old Radiator Company
Tenterden, United Kingdom
Specialized in the refurbishing of original cast-iron radiators.
___theoldradiatorcompany.co.uk

Tubes Radiatori
Resana, Italy
Radiators that are interior design elements rather than just system components.
___tubesradiatori.com

Modernist Modularity

Engaging with human hands multiple times a day, door handles are a necessary part of everyday life. So why is their design so often overlooked? The design studio of Manuel Bonnemazou and Agnès Cambus in Paris have taken up the task of remedying this; their modular concept revives the door handle genre with simple, bold design. Handle components in solid brass are handcrafted in Parisian workshops, and can be mixed and matched in a variety of shapes, colors, and finishes. Trained in industrial and interior design, Bonnemazou and Cambus got the idea for their product line while working on various architectural projects. According to the designers, "the door handle is an object often discussed at the end of the building site without any real identity. We wanted to imagine a concept that is part of the architectural project." ✗

Agnès Cambus and Manuel Bonnemazou work with Parisian artisans to produce their modular door handle system: five forms can be combined with three knobs and four collections of ornamental backplates.

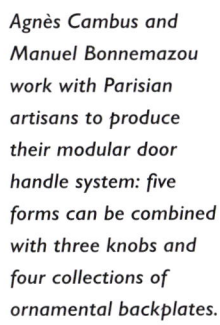

New Belgian Accents

"It was never the plan to become kitchen designers," emphasizes Pierric De Coster, who founded Atelier Dialect together with fellow architect Jonas Blondeel in 2012. The pair started with smaller furniture pieces after realizing they both love to study objects in detail and use a pared-back aesthetic. "Our furniture is there to make a room better but shouldn't demand all the attention," they say. After completing their first kitchen, the Belgians shifted their focus toward cabinetry. Word of mouth traveled fast, and after receiving more inquiries for kitchens, they changed their way of working. Not only is each bespoke design informed by the architecture, but the client also has an impact on the result: "I think we would never have had the idea of making a pink kitchen by ourselves. Here, the client suggested the color as a striking contrast to a very white apartment. And we took it from there." Always keen to try new things, the duo loves to experiment with materials, colors, and finishes. "That might mean some trial and error, but we're not afraid of that." ✕

Wood-Bending Beauty

Sensual and sinuous, the wooden creations of Joseph Walsh gracefully straddle the realms of art and furniture. Born in 1979 and based in Cork, Ireland, the self-taught designer crafts unique furniture, wall pieces, and sculptures that curve, twist, and join in the most remarkable ways. Ribbons of indigenous ash wood spiral into a tabletop or undulate into a chair, as if on the brink of evolving into a different organic shape at any moment. Walsh explores relationships between "the ordered and chaotic; the geometric and the lyrical," working with an international team of accomplished artisans and visiting consultants. They enrich the studio's expertise with skills such as computer-aided design, structural engineering, resin casting, stone carving, and upholstery. Walsh has described his work as "both a study and an expression of the relationship between the beauty we create, and the beauty we allow to happen; the beauty we participate in creating, and the beauty we quietly observe."

For the Enignum series (previous page), wood is first peeled into thin sheets then manipulated into free-form compositions. The living sculpture Lillium (left) develops the same technique towards purely playful and artistic ends, seen here in white oiled olive ash.

cc-tapis

Pile with Style

Far from mass production, Milan-based cc-tapis works with artisans in Nepal to explore new approaches to carpet making with respect to the materials and culture of this ancient craft.

The Quadro celeste rug is designed by Milanese agency Studiopepe (this page). cc-tapis creative director Daniele Lora with the founders Nelcya and Fabrizio Cantoni (left page).

All rugs are being produced by hand in an atelier on the outskirts of Kathmandu in Nepal. This involves the spinning of the yarns (top), to the colouring, knotting (bottom) and the finishing touches like hand-cutting (opposite above), shearing, and embossing.

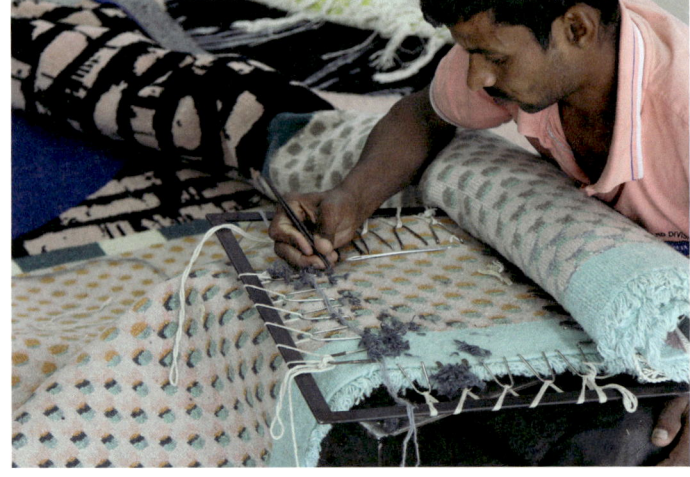

Part of the fun, when first visiting someone's home, is seeing how they have decorated the place. Well, and then, wondering if you would have made the same choices. Usually the eyes go straight to the walls, scrutinizing the artwork hanging there. Unless, of course, there is a rug by cc-tapis in the room. The modern, hand-knotted pieces made from fine yarns are joyful showstoppers, turning floors into canvases with their bold patterns and intense color combinations. Founded by wife and husband Nelcya and Fabrizio Cantoni, the Milan-based brand has shaken up the world of rugs since its relaunch in 2011. Inviting young designers as well as famous names to collaborate with them, cc-tapis has contributed to the recent renaissance of weaving as a craft.

Why did you feel the need for a reshuffle in 2011?
Well, we started cc-tapis in 2001 in Strasbourg with a shop where we sold contemporary rugs that we produced ourselves. That went pretty well. We even had clients in Paris—quite an achievement considering everything outside of the capital is seen as province. At one point Nelcya

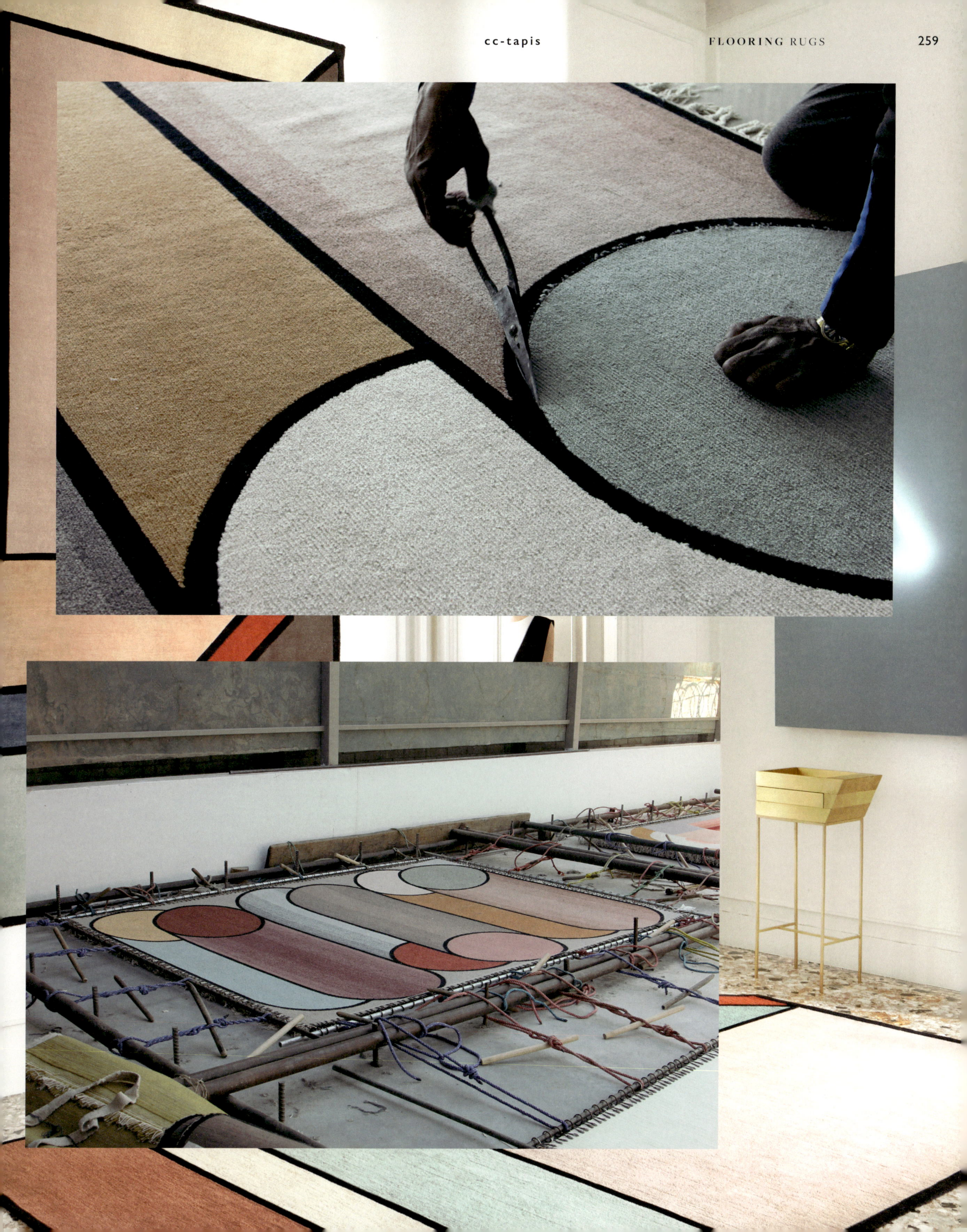

Italian-based designer Patricia Urquiola creates 3D-effects on a two-dimensional surface with her Rotazioni rugs (this page) and the Visioni range (right page) both knotted from Himalayan wool.

suggested—and I always listen to her—that we move to Milan. There I enrolled at the university to study interior design because I had never received a proper education in this field. Which was great; it dusted off my mind. This is also where I met Daniele Lora, who is now our art director. He impressed me with his typical Milanese *buon gusto*, which means he can take any project and transform it into something elegant. And the three of us decided, at some point, to relaunch cc-tapis and turn it into a distinctive brand.

How did you start this process of relaunching?
First, we found a space in Brera, and sold our house to pay for all of this. Then we needed to sort out production. Before, we worked with Indian manufacturers who are very nice people, but they outsource every step of the process. We would have had no control. So we moved to Nepal to found a company there with a local associate. That way we can do everything in-house in our own workshops. We buy the yarn and color it; we knot the rugs, do the finishings, and ship everything.

Why is that control so important to you?
It enables us to innovate. I will say this: you might not like the designs of our rugs—taste is subjective—but the quality in them isn't. We don't use acids, we don't use chemicals. We wash our rugs with purified rainwater. It is a very, very traditional approach to the craft. That said, we still want to bring in something new through the design and the knotting. What we try not to do is cheat, like using acids or shortcuts to gain an effect or a result on a rug.

Where do these new ideas come from?
When we started seven years ago with modern patterns, everybody was doing these scratched effects. Except for us. We did our bold patterns and mid-century-influenced designs. After doing all designs in-house, we were ready to open up to other interpretations. I think the best thing that happened to us back then was Patricia Urquiola. We met on a

The Eyes in Chains rug is designed by Milanese designer Federico Pepe (this page). The Hello Sonia wall hanging is by Studiopepe (right page top) and the Birth on the Dancefloor design by Marta Bagante (right page bottom).

project through a mutual friend and we entered the beautiful world of Patricia. She drew the Visioni rug range for us; it is this idea of playing with 3D, but on a 2D surface. We work with these great names who have a lot to teach us.

And how much do you teach the designers about rugs?
Nothing, that's the point. We like to work with people outside of the rug industry and with young designers who are totally free in their approach. Let them think, elaborate, and create. And afterwards, we see if we can do it. For example, Chiara Andreatti was inspired by the Wiener Werkstätte. For her design, we produced yarns and threads that were very large; and the rugs have a lower knot count. Due to the size of the thread, these designs, which are usually very, very neat, looked not so precise. And we worked in elements of flat weaves, which are normally very precise and flat. But with a yarn like that, the whole rug grows somehow.

What materials do you usually use for the yarns?
We use only Himalayan wool, instead of wool from New Zealand. I have nothing against New Zealand, but the wool from there is very plush, very soft. Beautiful for sweaters, but with rugs it absorbs the color in a way that is too uniform. When you knot it in the plain it is flat. Himalayan wool is different; it absorbs the color, leaving very natural, very, very light abrage—meaning the color's tonality changes in the yarn—which makes the rug real. We also weave with pure silk and aloe; the latter doesn't shed at all. And we started using linen when working with Faye Toogood, which has a certain quality reminiscent of silk, only it's not as shiny. There is a beautiful Italian word called *materico*, which means you can see the matter, the fine.

What care do rugs of this quality need?
Only common sense. You need to vacuum them, sometimes upside down so that you really clean the inside of the rug. Sometimes a bit of cold water, a neutral soap, and a brush will do the job. All these mechanical things or dry cleaners are not right for a rug. My advice: find a local traditional Persian rug dealer. They know a lot about the maintenance.

How does sunlight affect a rug? Is it very damaging to the colors?
You want the rugs to age gracefully and uniformly. If only one part of the rug is exposed—and by the way, the sun and the moon have the same effect—this side will age a bit more than the other. So I suggest turning it around once or twice a year. Then you will not even notice the slight changes in color. In the end, everything ages with light—even us.

Above, a handmade ceramic tile by German tile company Golem, a leading European producer of historic tiles, manufactured according to traditional techniques.

Art Nouveau Novelties

On the grounds of an old manor near Berlin, German company Golem recreates history with its handmade ceramic tiles. The company began in 1991 when ceramic artists Tomas Grzimek and Ulrich Schumann built up a small team to produce bricks and terracotta tiles for old East German villas and churches in need of restoration. In 2001, Grzimek and his wife, sculptor Sabine Heller, changed the company's focus and concentrated on the production of Art Nouveau (Jugendstil) tiles. Word of their skill soon spread among architects and restorers of the city's many listed properties, and today the company receives orders for replica and custom tiles from clients around the world. At Golem, where all work that can be done by hand is done according to traditional nineteenth century manufacturing techniques, time goes hand-in-hand with quality. One of the most modern aspects of the company is its kiln, which also works overnight to fire the hand-cast, hand-painted tiles. Says production manager Manfred Bierke, "If we used a machine, it wouldn't look the way it did two or three hundred years ago, and it wouldn't be as beautiful." ✕

With their distinctive crackle glaze (this page), Golem's Art Nouveau tiles are produced just as they were around the 1900s: molded or dust-pressed with embossed contour lines that are hand-filled with glaze using slip trailers (previous page).

Golem DECORATIONS TILES

Golem's palette of historic wall and floor tiles spans ornate Wilhelminian patterns, sinuous Art Nouveau motifs, geometric Art Deco forms, as well as modern designs.

Index

&tradition
Denmark
pp. 7 top right, 97 bottom, 148, 149 top
andtradition.com

Ailanto Design
Italy
pp. 192 bottom, 194 bottom
ailantodesign.com

Amy Somerville
United Kingdom
pp. 140–147, 150 top
amysomerville.com

Anchor Ceramics
Australia
pp. 136–139
Photography: Derek Swalwell (p. 136), Anchor Ceramics (pp. 137 top left, 139 top left and right), Tatjana Plitt (p. 137 top right), Lisa Cohen (pp. 137 bottom, 138, 139 bottom)
anchorceramics.com

Anna Karlin
United States
pp. 72–73
Photography: Jonathan Tasker
annakarlin.com

Atelier Dialect
Belgium
pp. 216, 250–251
Photography: Atelier Dialect (pp. 250, 251 bottom left and right), Robbie Depuydt (p. 251 top)
atelierdialect.be

Ateliers Zelij
France
pp. 212–215, 218 bottom
zelij.com

Bartmann Berlin
Germany
p. 151
bartmannberlin.de

Bloc Studios
Italy
pp. 5 bottom, 9 bottom, 97 top, 234–241, 243
Photography: Bloc Studios (pp. 5 bottom, 234–235, 237 top and bottom right, 238 left), Thevoz & Choquet (pp. 9 bottom, 97 top, 236, 237 bottom left, 238 right, 239), Nicola Gnesi (p. 235 right), Carl and Evelina Kleiner (pp. 240, 241 bottom), Pim Top (p. 241 top)
Design: Thevoz & Choquet (pp. 9 bottom, 97, 238, 239, 243), Carl Kleiner (pp. 240, 241 bottom), Sabine Marcelis (p. 241 top)
bloc-studios.com

Bonnemazou Cambus
France
pp. 246–249
Photography: Bonnemazou Cambus (pp. 246, 247 bottom), Romain Rivière (pp. 247 top left und right, 248), Marie Lukasiewicz (p. 249)
bonnemazou-cambus.fr

Braquenié
France
pp. 184–191
pierrefrey.com

cc-tapis
Italy
pp. 6 top, 29, 256–263
Photography: cc-tapis (pp. 6 top, 29, 256, 258, 259, 260 right, 263), Lorenzo Gironi (pp. 257, 260 left, 261, 262)
Art Direction: Studio Milo and Motel409 (pp. 257, 260 left, 261, 262)
Design: Studiopepe. (p. 257), Patricia Urquiola (pp. 260, 261), Federico Pepe (p. 262, 263 top), Marta Bagante (p. 263 bottom)
cc-tapis.com

Charles Dedman
United Kingdom
pp. 162–163
Photography: Charles Dedman
charlesdedman.co.uk

Clarence House
United States
pp. 104–107, 219 bottom
Photography: Clarence House
clarencehouse.com

Cristina Celestino
Italy
pp. 52–55, 242 bottom
Photography: Mattia Balsamini
Manufacturer: Botteganove (pp. 52 top, 53, 55), Fornace Brioni (pp. 52 bottom, 54)
cristinacelestino.com

Crosby Studios
United States
pp. 64–67
Photography: Lena Shkoda (pp. 64, 67 top), Evgeny Evgrafov (p. 65), Gleb Leonov (p. 66), Crosby Studios (p. 67 bottom)
crosby-studios.com

david/nicolas
Lebanon
pp. 116 top
Photography: Emanuele Tortora
davidandnicolas.com

Dinesen
Denmark
pp. 18–27, 28
Photography: Alf Jäger Arén (p. 18), Dinesen (pp. 19, 20, 21, 22, 23 bottom, 26, 27), Yuta Sawamura (p. 23 top) Anders Hviid/Dinesen (pp. 24, 28), Peter Krasilnikoff (p. 25)
Design: Anne-Karin Furunes und Kalle Eriksson (p. 18), OeO Studio (pp. 22 top, 23 top, 26), La'ket Arkitekten (pp. 22 bottom, 23 bottom), Maali & Lalanda Architects (p. 24), Studio David Thulstrup (p. 25), Anouska Hempel (p. 27)
dinesen.com

DWA Design Studio
Italy
pp. 128–131
Photography: Alberto Strada (pp. 128, 129, 131 top left and bottom), Italo Perna – Polifemo Fotografia (pp. 130, 131 top right)
Manufacturer: Mariotti Fulget Spa
dw-a.it

Eligo Studio
Italy
pp. 94–95
Photography: Delfino Sisto Legnani (p. 94), Tommaso Riva (p. 95 top left and bottom), Eligo Studio (p. 95 top right)
eligostudio.it

Ellisha Alexina
United States
p. 194 top
Photography: Joyelle West
ellishaalexina.com

Emery & Cie
Belgium
pp. 217, 245
emeryetcie.com

Emmanuelle Simon
France
p. 150 bottom
emmanuellesimon.com

Ferréol Babin
France
pp. 79 top, 115 bottom
Photography: Ferréol Babin
ferreolbabin.fr

Framework Studio
Netherlands
p. 244
Photography: Kasia Gatkowska
framework.eu

Friederike Tebbe
Germany
p. 219 top
farbarchiv.de

Fromental
United Kingdom
pp. 90–93, 195 bottom
fromental.co.uk

Garde Hvalsoe
Denmark
pp. 5 top, 154–157
Photography: Garde Hvalsøe (pp. 5 top, 154 top right and bottom, 156, 157), Karen Rosetztsky (p. 154 top left), Pernille Kaalund (p. 155)
Design: OeO Studio and Garde Hvalsøe (pp. 156, 157 top left)
gardehvalsoe.dk

Garnier & Linker
France
pp. 9 top, 117 bottom, 122–123
Photography: Garnier & Linker (pp. 9 top, 117 bottom, 122, 123 top and bottom right), Yannick Labrousse (p. 123 bottom left)
garnieretlinker.com

Geoffrey Preston Sculpture & Design
United Kingdom
pp. 4, 56–63, 81
Photography: Nick Carter (pp. 4, 56 bottom, 57, 59 top, 60 bottom, 61, 62, 63 bottom, 81), Mark Girvan (p. 56 top), Jenny Lawrence (pp. 58 top, 59 bottom, 60 top), Jason Ingram (p. 63 top left), Geoffrey Preston (pp. 58 bottom, 63 top right)
geoffreypreston.co.uk

Germans Ermičs
Netherlands
pp. 196–199
Photography: Jan Willem Kaldenbach (p. 196 top left), Floor Knaapen (p. 196 top right and bottom), Jussi Puikkonen (pp. 197, 198), Lonneke van der Palen (p. 199)
germansermics.com

Golem
Germany
pp. 218 top, 264–269

golem-baukeramik.de

Houlès
France
pp. 68–71, 192 top
Photography: Houlès (pp. 68, 69 bottom, 70 top left and right, 192 top), Mooxy Production (pp. 69 top left and right, 70 bottom, 71)

houles.com

Iacoli & McAllister
United States
pp. 8 top, 78

iacolimcallister.com

Jan Hendzel
United Kingdom
p. 114
Photography: Fergus Coyle

janhendzel.com

Jende Posamenten Manufaktur
Germany
pp. 132–135

jende-manufaktur.de

John Sankey
United Kingdom
pp. 96, 208–211
Photography: Jonathan Juniper

johnsankey.co.uk

Joogii
United States
p. 242 top
Photography: Damian James

joogiidesign.com

Jorge Penadés
Spain
pp. 80, 164–167
Photography: Boris Schipper (p. 164 top), Humberto Ribes (pp. 164 bottom, 166), Brenda Germade (pp. 80, 165, 167)

jorgepenades.com

Joseph Walsh
Irland
pp. 10–11, 252–255
Photography: Andrew Bradley

josephwalshstudio.com

Kobenhavns Mobelsnedkeri
Denmark
pp. 30–35
Photography: Line Thit Klein (pp. 30, 31, 32, 33 bottom left and right, 34–35), Københavns Møbelsnedkeri (p. 33 top)

kbhsnedkeri.dk

Kraud
Germany
p. 116 bottom
Photography: Katrin Lautenbach

kraud.de

Laboratorio Paravicini
Italy
pp. 168–171, 172
Photography: Laboratorio Paravicini

paravicini.it

La Manufacture Cogolin
France
pp. 12–17
Photography: La Manufacture Cogolin

manufacturecogolin.com

Lison de Caunes
France
pp. 115 top, 200–207
Photography: Lison de Caunes (pp. 115 top, 200–201, 202, 203, 205, 206), Gilles Trillard (pp. 200 left, 207), Xavier Béjot (p. 204)

lisondecaunes.com

llot llov
Germany
pp. 230–233
Photography: Ender Suenni (pp. 230, 231 top right and bottom right, 232, 233), llot llov (p. 231 top left)

llotllov.de

Marcin Rusak
United Kingdom
pp. 46–51, 79 bottom
Photography: Marcin Ruska Studio (pp. 46, 47 top right and bottom left, 48 bottom left, 49, 50, 51, 79 bottom), Kat Green (p. 47 top left), Pim Top (p. 48 top and bottom right)

marcinrusak.com

Marta Sala Éditions
Italy
pp. 8 bottom, 82–85, 149 bottom
Photography: Jonathan Frantini (pp. 8 bottom, 83, 84, 85, 149 bottom), Antoine Antoine Rozès (p. 82)

martasalaeditions.it

Muller van Severen
Belgium
pp. 118–121, 242 top

mullervanseveren.be

Porzellan Manufaktur Nymphenburg
Germany
pp. 7 top left, 173, 224–229
Photography: Nymphenburg (pp. 7 top left, 224–225, 225 right, 226 bottom right, 227, 228), Frank Stolle (pp. 173 226 top and bottom left, 229)
Design: Peter Rank (p. 229)

nymphenburg.com

RENS
Netherlands
pp. 124–127
Photography: Lisa Klappe (pp. 124 top, 125, 127 top and bottom left), Sanne Veltman (pp. 124 bottom left und right, 127 bottom right), RENS (p. 126)
Manufacturer: RENS & Desso (pp. 124, 127)

madebyrens.nl

Roi du Lac
Italy
pp. 158–161
Photography: Max Catena, Paolo Falcone, and Laura Sciacovelli

roidulac.co.uk

Roll & Hill
United States
pp. 74–77
Photography: Roll & Hill (p. 74 top), Joseph De Leo (p. 74 bottom left), Jeffrey Schad (pp. 74 bottom right, 75, 76, 77)
Design: Ladies & Gentlemen (p. 74 bottom left), Lukas Peet (p. 75), Jason Miller (p. 76), Bec Brittain (p. 77)

rollandhill.com

Savoir Beds
United Kingdom
pp. 178–183

savoirbeds.com

Schotten & Hansen
Germany
pp. 174–177

schotten-hansen.com

Sebastian Cox
United Kingdom
pp. 42–45
Photography: Giovanni Nardi for The American Hardwood Export Council (pp. 42, 43 bottom, 44 top), Sebastian Cox (p. 43 top), Arte Del Legno (p. 44 bottom), The Glenlivet (p. 45)

sebastiancox.co.uk

Soane Britain
United Kingdom
pp. 108–113

soane.co.uk

Tadeáš Podracký
Czech Republic
pp. 152–153

tadeaspodracky.com

The Nanz Company
United States
pp. 86–89

nanz.com

Valentin Loellmann
Netherlands
pp. 6 bottom, 98–103

valentinloellmann.de

Victoria Wilmotte
France
pp. 36–41
Photography: Fabien Breuil

victoriawilmotte.fr

Vonnegut/Kraft
United States
p. 117 top
Photography: The White Arrow Collaboration with Kneip

vonnegutkraft.com

Voutsa
United States
pp. 193, 195 top, 220–223
Photography: Chris Gloag (p. 220), Annie Schlechter Courtesy Brock Forsblom (pp. 193, 221), Voutsa (pp. 195 top, 222, 223)

voutsa.com

Insiders
& COMPANY
The New Artisans of Interior Design

This book was conceived, edited, and designed by Gestalten.

Edited by Robert Klanten and Sally Fuls

Preface by Sally Fuls
Interviews by Marius Thies
Short Profiles by Alisa Kotmair
Translation Preface by Jen Metcalf

Project Management by Cyra Pfennings

Design by Britta van Kesteren
Layout by Capucine Labarthe and Mona Osterkamp
Creative Direction of Design and Cover by Ludwig Wendt

Typefaces: Chap by Lauri Toikka & Florian Schick,
Freight by Joshua Darden and Gill Sans by Eric Gill

Cover photography Antea Brugnoni by Paolo Leone

Printed by Nino Druck GmbH, Neustadt/Weinstraße
Made in Germany

Published by Gestalten, Berlin 2018
ISBN 978-3-89955-936-1

© Die Gestalten Verlag GmbH & Co. KG, Berlin 2018
All rights reserved. No part of this publication may be reproduced or transmitted in any form or by any means, electronic or mechanical, including photocopy or any storage and retrieval system, without permission in writing from the publisher.

Respect copyrights, encourage creativity!

For more information, and to order books, please visit www.gestalten.com.

Bibliographic information published by the Deutsche Nationalbibliothek. The Deutsche Nationalbibliothek lists this publication in the Deutsche Nationalbibliografie; detailed bibliographic data are available online at http://dnb.d-nb.de.

None of the content in this book was published in exchange for payment by commercial parties or designers; Gestalten selected all included work based solely on its artistic merit.

This book was printed on paper certified according to the standards of the FSC®.